Are You the New Manager?

Techniques, Guidelines, and Strategies for a Successful First Year

Lee Bertrand
Robert Blanck

iUniverse, Inc.
Bloomington

ARE YOU THE NEW MANAGER?
TECHNIQUES, GUIDELINES, AND STRATEGIES FOR A SUCCESSFUL FIRST YEAR

Copyright © 2013 Lee Bertrand & Robert Blanck.

All rights reserved. No part of this book may be used or reproduced by any means, graphic, electronic, or mechanical, including photocopying, recording, taping or by any information storage retrieval system without the written permission of the publisher except in the case of brief quotations embodied in critical articles and reviews.

iUniverse books may be ordered through booksellers or by contacting:

iUniverse
1663 Liberty Drive
Bloomington, IN 47403
www.iuniverse.com
1-800-Authors (1-800-288-4677)

Because of the dynamic nature of the Internet, any web addresses or links contained in this book may have changed since publication and may no longer be valid. The views expressed in this work are solely those of the author and do not necessarily reflect the views of the publisher, and the publisher hereby disclaims any responsibility for them.

Any people depicted in stock imagery provided by Thinkstock are models, and such images are being used for illustrative purposes only.

Certain stock imagery © Thinkstock.

ISBN: 978-1-4759-8245-9 (sc)
ISBN: 978-1-4759-8244-2 (hc)
ISBN: 978-1-4759-8243-5 (e)

Library of Congress Control Number: 2013905626

Printed in the United States of America.

iUniverse rev. date: 4/16/2013

Authors' Foreword

I HAVE WORKED AS a manager in many diverse environments including manufacturing, aerospace engineering, university graduate degree programs, urban and regional planning, distribution centers, and private business consulting. Additionally, I have earned a Lean Six Sigma Black Belt. For thirty years I watched the actions and efforts of successful managers and managers who were failures. From these experiences I and Lee have assembled a set of observations that are common to those managers who were the most successful. This book provides the opportunity to share with you the principles that you can take on the journey to becoming a successful manager.

– Robert Blanck

MY EARLIEST EXPERIENCES WITH management as both a follower and a leader began on the family dairy farm, and then through working in the family excavating and construction business. I gained experience as a United States Marine Corps Officer and with years of banking, while concurrently working as an Adjunct College Professor and as Bachelor of Science in Business Degree Program Director. These life experiences exposed me to various managerial styles with their related successes and failures; plus I had my own opportunity to succeed and, at times, fail as a manager.

Over the years, the working-adult business students in my courses posed real-world management situations that needed solving, and I, as the enthusiastic instructor, obliged by providing direct, no-nonsense advice, usually with great results. These work environments have benefitted me by helping me to refine my knowledge and understanding of effective management strategies. I used this insight as Dean of the Institute of Management Accountants' Leadership Academy to develop and deliver leadership programs. All management experiences, whether as a leader or a follower, are opportunities for learning. May you learn from this book and use the knowledge and wisdom contained herein to succeed.

– Lee Bertrand

Lead or follow or get out of the way! – *Thomas Paine*

This quote by Thomas Paine was one of Lee Bertrand's favorites. I place the quote here in honor of Lee and the hard work he invested in this book.

Acknowledgements

LEE AND I WANT to acknowledge the following individuals who have contributed to the effort of shaping the content of this text:

To Ryan M Blanck, who as an English teacher holding a graduate degree in the field and is recognized for his contributions to the world of literature, labored over the drafts offering refinements to sentence and grammar structures. Thank you Ryan; you provided effort and suggestions to bring this text to its completed state.

To Dr. David Balch, thank you for years of friendship and sharing of teaching responsibilities at the University of Redlands. As an instructor, co-author of published articles of research in business management, and as an academic administrator you continually demonstrate the highest levels of teaching and administrative skills. Your unique course "Humor in the Workplace" provides fresh insights for managers in leading work groups.

To Vic Downing, President & CEO of Global Advantage Inc, a lifelong friend who introduced me to the writers David Gleicher, Jack Gibb, Richard Beckhard, Edgar Schein, Malcolm

Gladwell, and Jeffrey Pfeffer to name only a few. My own philosophy of management emerged from our many hours of conversation regarding your work in building extraordinary business leaders. I am sure that you will see many common principles woven through the pages of this text. Thank you Vic.

To Randon Blanck for book cover conceptual design and illustrative development. Thank you Randy for your creativity.

To the hundreds of graduate students of business who have entered our classes and conference rooms seeking to improve their managerial and financial decision making skills. You brought thought-provoking questions, presented challenges, and then put into practice solutions created in our classrooms.

A special acknowledgement to my co-author Lee Bertrand, who lost his heroic battle with cancer just as this book's final draft was being assembled. His vision and motivation kept the task of writing on course. This book is dedicated as a memorial to Lee and his family and for his tireless efforts in assisting young aspiring managers build their leadership skills and careers.

Dedication

THE SURVIVAL OF AN organization, its employees, its customers, it suppliers, its stakeholders, and its community rests on the shoulders of the managers and their minute-by-minute decisions. This book is written for the professional who sees the opportunity to be a manager as the greatest and most rewarding experience and challenge within modern business.

Table of Contents

Authors' Foreword v

Acknowledgements vii

Dedication ix

Introduction xvii
   Why this book xviii
   How to use this book. xviii

Getting Started 1
Step 1: Building a clean and organized work environment . 3
   Applying the 5S Principles 3
   Summarizing 5S Principles 7
Step 2: Knowing the employees. 8
   Shadowing 9
   Questioning while shadowing 10
   Making on the spot decisions 13
Step 3: Using "Open Door" management. 13
   Describing an open door visit 13
   Designing an effective open door approach 15

Step 4: Creating stability in the work environment 17
    Uncompromising attitude 18
    Creating a stable work environment 19
    Correcting an environment of confusion and uncertainty . . .21
    Understanding the root cause of an unstable environment . . .23
Step 5: Making the work area and employees mistake-proof. 24
    Describing Poka-Yoke methods 24
    Using Poka-Yoke in everyday life 25
    Incorporating Poka Yoke 26
Step 6: Writing a Code of Conduct for the Department . .26
    Reviewing a sample Code of Conduct 27
    Providing for a dynamic instrument. 28
Step 7: Selecting a management style 29
    Describing various styles 30
    Illustrating the styles. .31
    Assembling an eclectic management style. 32
Step 8: Producing productive staff meetings. 33
    Preparing the first meeting 33
    Creating meeting structure 34
    Producing the meeting's final product 41
    Managing the meeting schedule 41
    Listing meeting action items. 44
Step 9: Writing the first set of Critical Success Factors. . .45
    Defining a Critical Success Factor 45
    Writing the Critical Success Factors 48
    Teaching employees to measure their own efforts 49
Step 10: Discovering and evaluating group's informal leaders. 50
    Discovering why informal leaders exist 50
    Describing an informal leader 51
    Ferreting out and neutralizing the informal leader's impacts. .53

 Understanding the informal leader's goals and attitudes 54
 Getting the informal leader to acknowledge department
  leadership. 54

Measuring Performance as a Manager 57
Checking first month of performance. 57
 Measuring the Critical Success Factors 58
 Checking what should have happened and creating a repair list 59
 Building a "shock absorber" attitude between the
  employees, the supervisor, and the customers 60
 Planning for next year's performance review 62
 Setting up the accountability meeting with the supervisor . . .63
Checking the first six months and measuring the Critical
 Success Factors 63
 Getting ready for the first formal performance appraisal . . .64
 Establishing goals and accountabilities for the employees . . .65
Checking the first year of performance 66
 Setting performance goals for the first year 67
 Rating the first year by looking in the rear-view mirror. . . .69
 Repeating the first year again or starting a new second year . .70
 Keeping the supervisor on track and managing the supervisor 73
Evaluating the organization, division, section, or department
 – a better place because of the year you invested 73
 Evaluating performance from a historical perspective 73

Adding Skills and Capabilities as a Manager 75
Coaching employee performance. 75
Managing using diagnostic skills 76
 Recognizing symptoms and prescribing treatment for a
  diseased organization. 76
 Defining a healthy organization 77
 Planning to heal a diseased organization 78

- *Training the employees to recognize an organizational disease and then produce their own treatment plan* 83
- Conducting performance review meetings with the employees 83
  - *Designing an employee performance review meeting* 85
  - *Anticipating the two different points of view* 85
- Recognizing conflict within the work group 87
  - *Understanding why conflict exists* 87
  - *Seeing opportunity vs. danger* 88
  - *Recognizing the various levels of conflict.* 89
- Keeping support staff supportive 92
  - *Building relationships with support staff.* 92
  - *Giving support staff an opportunity to contribute to the team environment* 92
- Finding humor in the workplace 93
- Preparing the employees for bigger and better opportunities. 94
  - *Helping the employees build careers.* 94
  - *Producing superior performers developing employees who will leave.* 96
- Hiring new employees 97
  - *Finding the right employee, or just filling the spot for now and hoping for the best* 97
  - *Interviewing process* .99
- Letting employees go. 101
  - *Taking disciplinary steps* 102
  - *Terminating procedures* 104
  - *Controlling unemployment benefits.* 105
- Managing a process and a project 106
  - *Defining Process Management.* 106
  - *Defining Project Management* 107
  - *Summarizing Process Management and Project Management* 116

Building a Career 119
Using a mentor. 119
Getting a ticket punched in the organization 120
    Finding career ladders and glass ceilings 121
    Finding technical training – job performance enhancement . 122
    Measuring the value of education for the working adult. . . 123
Networking and career growth 125
    Using professional associations and memberships –
        purpose and opportunities 125
    Networking within a professional association 126
    Listing of a few professional associations. 127
Discovering that a career ladder is leaning against the wrong
    building 128
    Producing the plan. 128
    Getting organized – a preparatory step 129
    Preparing a custom-designed resume 129
    Completing the corporate financial research. 131
    Completing the corporate publicity research. 132
    Getting through a successful interview. 132
    Considering the key points in the interview 135

Stocking the Manager's Tool Box 137
Applying strategic change. 137
    Facing the most difficult task – accomplishing change . . . 138
    Managing and being a change agent 139
Applying Lean Six Sigma and Continuous Quality
    Improvement. 140
    Defining Lean Six Sigma 140
    Defining Six Sigma. 141
    Summarizing Lean Six Sigma 143
Observing an organization's culture. 143
    Listing of the symbols of organizational culture 143

    Studying the elements of organization culture. 146
Looking at successful organizations 147
    Measuring the seven practices of successful organizations . . 147
    Evaluating a group's effectiveness and maturity 148
Interviewing applicants for management positions 150
Measuring personal value systems 152

Conclusion 155

Appendix 157
Classic writings 157
Resource materials 160
    Appendix A – Business and management journals 161
    Appendix B – Business magazines and newspapers 163
    Appendix C – Business and management books 165
    Appendix D – Professional Associations 167
Citations 171

Introduction

IN PURCHASING THIS BOOK, you have expressed interest in learning about the function of management and the task of planning, organizing, directing, and controlling the work of others who report to you. This book describes the steps that, when applied, will establish high levels of employee productivity and morale.

Over a lifetime of work, personal experiences as a manager will give you a broad perspective, but now is the time to build skills. In most cases, managers use those experiences as a lens to review their past performance. They are critical of themselves and ask two important questions: "Why did I do that?" And, "Why didn't I do this?" Often these experienced managers wish they could go back in time and counsel themselves to prevent career-altering mistakes and lost opportunities.

> "First rule of leadership: everything is your fault."
>
> - A Bug's Life

In this book you will in effect be time traveling because you will have two experienced managers observing and whispering advice through the words on the pages that follow. Two guys who have had significant successes, made mistakes, observed the successes of others and themselves, and compiled that information here for you to use.

In the Marines, they have a saying, "Lead by the numbers until you understand what you are doing." The numbers are identified tasks of leadership and planning that work well; we provide them here for you to consider.

Once you have read and pondered this book, do not be a hesitant leader; seek to solve problems and resolve situations. Fellow managers, rivals and employees will place obstacles in your path and present complex problems; adapt and overcome them.

Why this book

We have written this book because people who are now in management need a "how to do it book" containing proven strategies and advice. This book can be thought of as a directory or a repair guide for getting the job done.

How to use this book

This book has sections describing the skills needed for a manager to be successful the first year. It should be used as guide for conducting a successful staff meeting, writing a performance review, setting performance goals, and holding oneself and others accountable.

The table of contents pages provides detailed listing of all of the subjects addressed in the text. Review the chapter and topic headings – find an area of interest and try out the concepts. Locate an area that you feel best describes opportunities where you want to improve. We offer to you as a brand new manager the first ten steps to building a productive team, Example; you have been assigned an additional task of being a manager of a complex short term project. In that section you will find a listing of critical decisions you will face. In another area the steps to prepare for your first annual performance review are highlighted. Perhaps the existing staff meetings are a sore spot for the employees, check our suggestions to change the meeting environment. Use the table of contents listing to pick areas for quick review or serious study.

Getting Started

I WAS HIRED FOR my first management position, overseeing a conference center in the mountains of Southern California. About two days after starting the job, after I had settled into my office and gotten the lay of the land, I closed my office door and sat down at my desk as a startling revelation came over me: I was in charge. The buck stopped with me. I had the final say. There was no one to go to when the stuff hit the fan. It was all on my shoulders.

I made it through my first weeks and months as the new manager and facility administrator. I had my share of successes and failures. I wish I had had someone to come alongside me in that moment of panic and assure me everything would work out all right. The hope in writing this book is to provide you – the new manager – with the advice that I wish I had received during that first week on the job.

> "A rock pile ceases to be a rock pile the moment a single man contemplates it, bearing within him the image of a cathedral."
>
> - Antoine de Saint-Exupery

As a new manager, you are faced with the prospects of establishing a position of authority, developing creditability, mastering technical skills, and earning the respect of the employees who will be reporting to you. And, you have approximately one week to accomplish all this.

Before you get started, we have one strong caution: do not try to be a friend to the employees. They have friends; they want you to be their leader. The buck stops with you. If you have a panic attack, have it out of sight of the employees. Do not tell the employees your troubles; as far as they are concerned you have no troubles. If you need to talk with someone, talk with a peer, or better yet, a spouse or a close friend. If you have an unresolved personal issues, see a counselor and get them fixed. Do not share your personal issues with the employees!

If you do not have high moral standards, develop them. As you rise toward the top of the organization, more and more of your behavior will become public. Leaders are often toppled by a secret vice. If a behavior cannot stand the light of day, do not do it. Using recreational drugs, imbibing too much alcohol, or having affairs with fellow employees can never be considered acceptable behavior. Whether man or woman, you are a leader of truth and soberness. Plus, integrity and honesty will forever prosper.

Devalue personal standards and you will fail; there is no going back. White-collar criminals in prison are often interviewed about their misdeeds. They start out by saying "I am an honest person; I do not know how I got here." We do, if you break one legal or moral rule you will break another. However, it may appear that the organization is rewarding you for cutting corners and breaking a few rules, and they sing praises of your exceptional performance. But as soon as trouble hits, when questionable practices are exposed and the investigations begin, they will cut you off and even testify against you to save themselves. There is an old saying; ***"If they will cheat with you, they will cheat on you."*** Or put a different way, ***"Never risk yourself morally or ethically for the team."***

As you practice good leadership, you may discover that your organization's ethics do not line up with your standard. You have to make a choice, do you stay or go? Do not delude yourself into thinking that you can change the organization by setting the good example. The organization will more than likely change you into its likeness rather than the other way around. To maintain personal values you will have to move on. The sooner you move, the sooner life will be back on track and your own Code of Conduct reestablished.

> "I'm an optimist in the sense that I believe humans are noble and honorable, and some of them are really smart. I have a very optimistic view of individuals."
>
> - Steve Jobs

Enough philosophizing, let's get started and work through the first week:

As a new manager, two tasks need to be placed on the first week's calendar for execution: The first is to evaluate and create a clean and organized work environment. The second task is to get to know your employees.

STEP 1: BUILDING A CLEAN AND ORGANIZED WORK ENVIRONMENT

Applying the 5S Principles

In the wild, the alpha male of the pack must assert and maintain his dominance. He marks his territory and shows the rest of the pack that he is in charge. He sets the tone for the rest of the pack. As a new manager, you must establish your territory by creating clean and organized workspaces for the employees. Accomplish this task using the 5S principles shown below.[1] The term "5S" derives from the Japanese words for the five practices leading to a clean and manageable work area.

This author once observed a new department manager that came in the weekend before he was due to start work and spent hours cleaning his new office, establishing his territory and setting the tone for the start of his tenure. Then upon the arrival of the employees on Monday he provided the simple description of creating a 5S work environment using the newly cleaned office as an example.

You as the new manager have to establish your territory and set a 5S example for the employees. The next step is to give the employees the chance to own this new approach to organizing their workspaces. Each step, when followed, produces a new pride in the work place. Once 5S is implemented and sustained, the employees find their daily tasks easier and they work more efficient. The clutter is gone and all the tools and supplies are readily accessible.

Step	Japanese	Literal Translation	English
1	*Seiri*	Cleaning Up	Sorting
2	*Seiton*	Organizing	Straightening
3	*Seisi*	Cleaning	Shining
4	*Seketsi*	Standardizing	Standardizing
5	*Shitsuke*	Training & Discipline	Sustaining

Sorting – Keep what is needed

Decide what is needed in the workspace to accomplish the daily tasks.

Definition: To separate the necessary from the unnecessary items.
- Store often-used items in the work area.
- Move infrequently used items away from the work area and dispose of the remainder unused materials or supplies.
- Discuss removal of items with all employees to ensure that you and they see the value in the discarding process.

Benefits: Creates a safer work area. Gains space. It becomes easier for you to visualize the workflow and for employees to find often-used tools and supplies.

Straightening – Arrange necessary items

Arrange what is needed to accomplish the daily tasks.

Definition: To arrange all necessary items.
- Create a designated place for everything and put everything in its place.
- Arrange items so they are easily seen and accessible.
- Label the locations with shelf or cabinet tags or nameplates.
- Use a pegboard for hanging small hand tools such as scissors, rulers, pliers, screwdrivers, etc. and paint an outline of the tool under each peg on the board.
- Place resupplied stock into the designated location.
- Create green, yellow, and red tags for each storage location.
  - Green – existing supply of stock is adequate for the near future.
  - Yellow – stock is getting low and time to reorder.
  - Red – out of stock and current tasks cannot be completed.

Benefits: Saves time by reducing effort to find frequently used and needed items. A quick visual survey of the work area will indicate what supplies need to be reordered. Missing tools will easily be identified upon a quick look at the pegboard and the empty spaces.

Shining – Clean the workplace

Keep everything clean.

Definition: To clean everything and find ways to keep it clean. Cleaning is an important task to be accomplished every day.

- A clean workplace is a precursor to building a quality product and process.
    Dust, dirt, and waste materials cause product contamination, potential health hazards, and will slow productivity.
- A clean workplace helps to quickly identify abnormal conditions.
- A clean environment carries over into the quality of the work produced.

Benefits: Employee stress is reduced. Group morale and productivity improves.

Standardizing – Create consistency

Create a consistent approach for carrying out tasks.

Definition: Maintain the workplace activity at a level that uncovers problems and makes them obvious to all employees. This leads to continuous improvement of the work environment through the process of ongoing assessment and corrective action.

- Sustain the steps of sorting, straightening, and shining activities every day.
- Create and use visual controls which may consist of signboards, painted lines, pegboards, labeling, color coding strategies to maintain the established order.

Benefits: Keep the work area neat enough for visual

identifiers to be effective in uncovering problems. Adopt a system that enables all employees in the work area to identify problems when they occur and propose solutions.

Sustaining – Maintaining the 5S approach to management of the work area

Create a disciplined and committed group of employees for the 5S process. This is the essential first step toward becoming a manager.

Definition: To maintain discipline and the need to practice "sustaining" until it becomes a way of life

- Develop schedules and checklists that document procedures and workplace behavior. Some identify the checklists as *Standard Operating Procedures* or *SOPs*.
- Follow the schedules and checklists. Revise schedules and checklists as needed.
- Inspect the department area to ensure that the 5S is being maintained by the employees. *The employees only respect what you inspect.* Take a moment to plan for the start of the next week. Have each member of the team contribute to cleaning the common area first and then individual areas or workstations.

Benefits: Effort has been invested, the employees have worked hard, and now it is time to make sure the effort is maintained and the work environment improvements will continue.

Summarizing 5S Principles

About 30 minutes before the end of the day, walk the area, find something wrong, and tell the team to correct it. Just before quitting time, gather employees together and quickly summarize what the expectations are for the next day. As time goes on it will be more difficult for you to find something wrong, out of place or soiled. At some point, you will not find anything wrong then you say, "Good job." You will hear high fives as you leave; do not smile but keep walking.

When you get home laugh and enjoy the sweet feeling of a successful day and the implementation of a painless, positive significant strategic change to the work area. The changes will produce the benefits of creating a safe and clean area for the employees.

Benefits: Keep the 5S program vital in your work area. It creates a cleaner environment and a safer workplace. It contributes positively to how you and the employees will feel about the product being produced, about themselves, and the organization. You and the employees will take pride in the tasks-at-hand and their workplace, producing improved job satisfaction while quality becomes the center point.

The neighboring managers will be stopping by to inspect the improvements and the resulting increases in operating efficiencies. Soon they will be asking you for advice. Do not be surprised – you and the work group are getting noticed and setting the standard! This quite an accomplishment for being on the job for only one week!

STEP 2: KNOWING THE EMPLOYEES

An important, immediate task during this first week is to get to know each employee. You will be introduced to a number of people, some so high up in the organization that they will barely remember you. With each introduction, use the name three times. When you get a moment, write down identifiers and impressions of each person you meet. The key is to remember all of the names!

It is time to implement the "getting to know you" program. Here you build trust and mutual respect with your employees.

The best approach is to "shadow" each employee. A good starting point is to obtain job descriptions and job titles for each employee. These may already be on file in department administrative files. If not, check with HR and obtain copies. The point is to be able compare the employees' responses to your questions with the tasks defined for them in the job descriptions. Do not be surprised if current job descriptions are not available. Creating job descriptions will be a task you likely will have to put on the calendar. Eventually it is important to determine the degree to which your employees' daily assignments fit their defined tasks. If there is a mismatch you will have to work to bring it all into alignment – another future task.

Shadowing

Shadowing requires that you spend time with each employee. Here you observe the employee's workday without judging or correcting. Observe the simplicity and complexity of their daily tasks. Take notes. And be an attentive listener, it is their time to talk. Start at the top; shadow the direct reports first. Be friendly but not too friendly. Encourage them to talk. You will be told of the problems encountered; absolutely do not promise to fix anything, just tell them that you will look into it. When finished shadowing, you will be able to put their comments, problems and observations into perspective.

> "In the past a leader was a boss. Today's leaders must be partners with their people... they no longer can lead solely based on positional power."
>
> - Ken Blanchard

When all employees have been shadowed, take time to

organize your notes and create summaries. During the course of the conversations, private and unsolicited personal information may be shared with you. Confidences must be maintained. Later on when you are making decisions and actively managing to solve the identified problems keep in mind the level of trust you fostered. Some employees' problems cannot be solved, some will require HR intervention, and some issues will test and push your management skills to the limit. The critical point of this shadowing exercise is that you are taking the time to visit all employees at their workstations, observed their daily routines, listen and hear the stories of their successes, issues, and problems.

Questioning while shadowing

Now, let us return momentarily to the concept of "shadowing." There are questions to ask employees and things to quietly observe as you shadow them.

The following list of questions is provided for you as a shadowing guide. Some questions may not be appropriate for your group. Other questions can be held for future meetings. You will probably want to add a few of your own. This list is just a starting point:

> How long have you worked in this department and for the company?
>
> How were you selected for your current position?
>
> How are various tasks and responsibilities assigned to you?
>
> How do you use the available tools and resources to perform daily tasks?

How do you collaborate with others in and outside of the department in accomplishing the required work?

How are the products produced by you and the other employees received by the customer?

How is the quality the group's work measured? Does the measurement scale seem appropriate? Are the measurements of quality publically displayed?

How have you been trained to perform the tasks required of you? Was the training adequate?

How much pressure do you feel to perform the required tasks?

How much flexibility is given to you in executing the tasks?

How often during a day do you face a change in task or performance requirements?

Are those changes part of a normal routine?

Are the changes appropriate?

What do you see as the department and the organization's greatest strengths and weaknesses?

What are you actively involved in to improve the productivity and quality of the work performed?

What is the one thing about the assigned job that you like the most? What are you most proud of?

What is the one thing that you dislike the most? What causes the most frustration?

If you could change anything about the job or work environment what would it be?

Look through the list above and select a few questions that will help you to understand the tasks the employees are performing and their value to the organization. Put your selected questions in order from the simple to the complex.

When you have finished shadowing the employees assemble all of the notes. You are ready to begin the analysis of their answers with their job descriptions From this analysis you are prepared to appreciate the complexities of employees' work and your responsibilities as their manager.

The shadowing exercise will give you a valuable perspective on each employee and the work they accomplish. Most importantly is that you have shown a personal interest in each employee. The insight and goodwill gained will be invaluable to you as you shape the team. In the most immediate sense, you have fairly measured their workload. But more importantly you have, through the eyes of employees, gained an appreciation for the requirements of the customers to which the department delivers its finished product. From the shadowing you observed the interpersonal relationships among the members of the group. Seen the strengths of team and felt their attitudes regarding productivity. Witnessed the daily deadlines and gained an improved understanding of their interpretation of the production of quality work.

In some cases you will be told of their intentions and desires to move up and out of the department. Tread carefully here; just listen, do not promise, and do not offer advice, but do acknowledge their goals. This will be the opportunity for you to anticipate providing future career counseling and guidance. After you become familiar with the employees' performance records, your organization's policies regarding transfers, promotions, and resignations you can begin offering career guidance. Again the information must be kept in confidence. The goal is to listen; actions will come later.

Making on the spot decisions

During the first week avoid on-the-spot decisions! Decisions take time; information has to be gathered and organized. In reality, the suggestions made by employees often contain the best solutions to the problems you face as manager. A prepared leader needs to hear the shared information and weigh the suggestions with caution. In time and with experience you will be able to address each item presented to you. Even when the right decisions are made, correct actions taken, and in the end you will need to realize that all employees will not be satisfied. But you will have taken a significant step this first week in achieving the earned respect that will carry you through the tough times that await you.

STEP 3: USING "OPEN DOOR" MANAGEMENT

By completing **Step 2** above, "getting to know the employees," or shadowing you have successfully set the stage to create an "open door management" work atmosphere. While spending time with the employees and visiting in their workspaces you established a foundation and an atmosphere of interest, trust, and mutual respect. Here you learned each employee's history, the things that frustrate them, and the accomplishments of which they are most proud. Now it is their turn to come to visit you.

Describing an open door visit

The **Open Door** approach requires you to be a sympathetic listener, a sound and effective decision maker, and a creator of solutions to apparently unsolvable problems. Build the Open Door atmosphere based on trust, fairness, confidentiality, and ethical decision-making. If you do, each employee will realize that your office door is open and you are available to listen, to provide reflective feedback, to counsel, and to give simple and precise directions. The employees want to place their trust in you and seek your wisdom and problem-solving skills. There will be times when employees who work for other managers may stop by to visit. Give each employee the opportunity to talk as time permits.

We caution you not to break the chain of command during this process of listening to employees outside of your department. After meeting with an employee outside of your work group you should consider informing the employee's immediate supervisor. This step will allow the supervisor to be aware of the conversation; its content and issues that may have been raised. In some cases the employee's request for confidentiality of the conversation may have to be respected. The decision to tell or not to tell the employee's supervisor is a personal decision you will have to make.

> "Leadership is solving problems. The day soldiers stop bringing you their problems is the day you have stopped leading them. They have either lost confidence that you can help or concluded you do not care. Either case is a failure of leadership."
>
> - Colin Powell

Designing an effective open door approach

The secret to effective **Open Door** policy: each employee deserves and receives undivided attention – no answering phone calls or emergency e-mails, or allowing interruptions. Each meeting you have continues to build trust, confidentiality, and sincerity within the employees that report to you. The "open door" attitude is maintained every day by ensuring that the employees know their work and well-being is your highest priority. As a reminder, all meetings with your employees must be confidential. Once the meeting begins the room door is closed and locked if necessary.

In each meeting, you have the opportunity to show the employee how their daily activities fit into the business plan for the whole organization. Show them that their work needs to provide the customers with the best product possible, and how their day-to-day activities contribute to the productivity and profitability of the organization. In addition, you have the opportunity to demonstrate your support for the employee.

> "Power isn't control at all — power is strength, and giving that strength to others. A leader isn't someone who forces others to make him stronger; a leader is someone willing to give his strength to others that they may have the strength to stand on their own."
>
> - Beth Revis

It is essential that you guard against showing favoritism. Favoring the advice of one employee over another destroys the group's internal working relationships. Everyone's concerns and comments must get a fair hearing. You do not have to take their advice, nor apologize for not taking it. Concerns have to be dealt with.

Do not develop pet subordinates; it is not good for them or for you. Ensure that all who meet with you will receive a fair amount of time.

There will be times when you have to close and lock your office door to in order to have a quiet time to finish a project, complete a conference call, or just take time to think through a complex issue. The employees will respect your locked office door; they understand the value of quiet time too. The Open Door policy is still in place, but you will meet with the employees at a later time.

Invariably, you will spend more time with those whom you like. But often times, it is not the one whom you like that is the good employee; it's the one who annoys you with uncomfortable observations and difficult suggestions. The rule of thumb is that those that do not mesh with you on a personal level often have the greater value to you and the organization than those with whom you get along. Your social skills in dealing with all employees will be tested, but regardless their improved work performance is always the ultimate goal.

The author served for twelve years as a high school principal and shares the following experience. The student population and parents were very diverse. Some parents could not be satisfied with the school's operating policies and procedures. At times confrontations occurred between the parents and teachers and office staff. Parent committees were formed to provide parents opportunities for participation in campus administration. The most "troublesome" parents were offered the first set of opportunities to serve on the advisory committees.

In this process of getting the parents involved, the most remarkable transformation took place. The parents became the school's most loyal supporters, offered credible suggestions and defended the school during the Accreditation Visiting Team inspection of the campus. The credibility of the school and its programs increased substantially as the parents were now actively promoting and defending the administrative processes. There's an old saying that goes, "Keep your friends close, but keep your enemies even closer."[2]

Lastly, high maintenance employees' will feast on available attention; you will have to control them by saying "no" occasionally and maintaining a comfortable distance. The key is consistency in decision-making. The same situation must receive the same response from you regardless of who presents it or how it is presented.

Step 4: Creating stability in the work environment

"Mean what you say and say what you mean!"[3] as found in the 1940 classic children's story *Horton Hatches the Egg* by Dr. Seuss.

By being an effective manager the employees can trust you to do what you say. They can take you at your word; if you say it, it's going to happen. You have built trusting relationships with the employees by shadowing them and using an open door management style. However, the employee must understand that if they share anything during a conversation you have with them that describes violations of company policies, criminal acts, endangerment of the safety of other

> "Think twice before you speak, because your words and influence will plant the seed of either success or failure in the mind of another."
>
> - Napoleon Hill

employees or has actually caused injuries, production of inferior product that could impact health or safety of a customer, civil torts, or violation of personal rights, then you will have no alternative but to inform the employee that you must pursue the situation to its final resolution. Matters of such nature cannot be covered up, disguised, or casually brushed aside. The situation has to be presented to the next higher level manager, the HR and Legal Departments, and statements from witnesses may be needed. At this point HR, and Legal Departments will take the lead. Be careful and be prepared the situation can turn sour very quickly.

This phrase may become a personal experience for you: **"Don't shoot the messenger"** was first expressed by Shakespeare in Henry IV, part 2 (1598) and in Antony and Cleopatra: when Cleopatra is told Antony has married another. Prior to that, a related sentiment was expressed in Antigone by Sophocles as **"No one loves the messenger who brings bad news."** Be prepared for the worse; maintain a secure personal documentation file of all of the events and conversations related to the sensitive situation. Some complex situations will take time to resolve. Plan for the worst and hope for the best. This situation may be the challenge that becomes the tipping point for your career as the new manager.

Uncompromising attitude

You have created an atmosphere based upon an uncompromising attitude of honesty, sincerity, confidentiality, and integrity. Replies couched in truth and sincerity may and probably will cause you short-term pain but soon the air will clear and work will continue. The long-term goal: Integrity and honesty must prevail. The following quote from **Marmion** by Sir Walter Scott seems to fit this perfectly: **"Oh what a tangled web we** *weave, when first we practice to deceive!"* Dishonestly of any kind – even a "little white lie" – will eventually come around and get you in the end. The truth will eventually come out, and the reputation and the respect you have worked so hard to gain may be lost. As Mark Twain once said – "If you tell the truth, you don't have to remember anything." This simple set of eleven words must be a guide for all of your interactions with others.

Creating a stable work environment

The previous manager in the department may have left you with an environment where decisions were not consistent, employees remained in a state of confusion, and the workday was unpredictable. This is the antithesis of a stable, predictable workplace that you now have the challenge of establishing.

You may have inherited an unstable department or unit. There is a recommended approach to re-stabilize your work group. The following discussion presents a set of suggested steps needed to create or recreate stability within the work group and in the relationships with the employees.

The first step is for you to **share information** regarding the specific situation and present your expectations to the employees. For example, employees will be presenting you with questions, concerns that are couched in an underlying feeling of frustration and confusion. These small issues may be irritating to you, but each must be addressed because you are creating within each employee the first step of establishing a stable and predictable work setting. Their questions deserve to be heard and addressed!

The second step requires that you establish your role as manager and **gain the mutual commitment** from the employees involved in the tasks at hand. As you answer each of their questions, they soon begin to realize that you are committed to being their manager, committed to answering their questions, and committed to making their day productive. Thus, you are clarifying and creating a managerial role by providing the extra time and effort to clarify each of their questions. The steps of shadowing and open door managerial approach are now being brought home as you seek to establish a stable work environment for your employees.

In following these two steps discussed above, a condition of **stability** in the work area can be created. However another simple question or minor confusion usually surfaces among the employees. This can represent a simple misunderstanding or a question. For example, upper management may make a change to the company dress code which you will have to communicate to your group. When presenting this change to employees, one may ask why the change was made and why employees are being told to adapt. Do not consider the question as a direct challenge to your authority, because that is likely not the employee's intention. The employee is seeking information do not consider it a challenge.

If you take the question as a challenge and become defensive, then you will appear to be insecure with the situation and quickly lose the respect of the employees. Each question or request for clarification must be addressed in a positive manner. When a question arises return to the first step to restate the clarifying information, expectations, and commitment to the policies or procedures and to the employees' success; answer the question as needed. Be careful in formulating the answer. Do not answer the unasked question! Do not look for complexity. If you are unsure of the question ask for a clarification then provide a simple answer.

Continue through these two steps of the clarification cycle

until **stability** is once again reestablished. Non-confrontational handling of these simple levels of confusion or questions will determine the success of your management goal to create a **stable** and predictable work environment. Once you feel comfortable with the two steps for creating a predictable and stable work environment, you will be able to identify the root causes of previous levels of conflict and be able to successfully create solutions and restore a sense of **stability** in the work environment.

Correcting an environment of confusion and uncertainty

However, there will be occasions when the employee's question or confusion will slip past you and the confusion is mistakenly ignored by you. That outcome or situation may produce levels of conflict, anger, and resentment within the work group or between you and the employees. The solutions to such situations are often complex and very emotionally draining for you and the employees involved. Steps to repair the complex situations are offered below.

> "The productivity of a work group seems to depend on how the group members see their own goals in relation to the goals of the organization."
>
> - Ken Blanchard

You must recognize the feelings of anger, frustration, resentment or ambiguity being held among the employees. At this point with the feeling of **stability** gone there are only three options or courses of action available to you. All three require the expenditure of a lot of your emotional energy to regain the desired **stability**.

Of the three options, the most destructive is the **first: "hostile termination of the relationship**." Here you and the employee dissolve the professional relationship. The employee may request a transfer, may resign, or otherwise may be removed from the work setting. Nothing was gained, all has been lost, and the environment has fostered a destructive and unproductive atmosphere. The feelings of conflict, anger, and resentment among other employees may remain and can linger for weeks or months.

A **second: "pull rank;"** that is, you declare your position as their manager, choose to ignore their feelings, and press on with the tasks at hand. Here you are commanding their commitment to the task Employees' feelings of conflict, anger, and resentment continue to fester. The need for a hostile termination of the relationships will now be more intense. Nothing has been gained; all has been lost.

A **third: renegotiation of expectations under duress,** is the most demanding but produces healing and reconstruction of the relationships within your work group. Under the burden of the extreme feelings of conflict, anger, and resentment you must assemble the group and begin again with the process of the first step sharing information, establishing expectations, listening to their expectations, reviewing their roles and regaining commitment. Here you give employees time to drain their feelings of conflict, anger, and resentment, heal the open wounds, and regain faith and interpersonal trust within the work group. Again the larger goal is to seek, reestablish, and then maintain a **stable** and predictable work environment for all of your employees.

Once the feelings of anger, resentment, and frustration have dissipated the next goal is to monitor the **stable** environment, waiting for the next question or state of confusion to occur. And, the repair process is again put into play. The repair process may need to be implemented daily at the beginning of your term as manager. As time passes and the employees' confidence in you grows the need for repairing will decline.

Understanding the root cause of an unstable environment

As the manager you must be aware that the root cause of some unstable work environmental conditions rests with a mismatch between an employee and the goals of the department and or the organization. The employee may be highly qualified and be well liked by the coworkers, but might simply be a bad fit for the department. The lingering levels of conflict, confusion, frustration, and at times anger must be dwelt with. During the shadowing of the employees you probably identify such conditions left over from the previous manager or that are produced by existing organizational regulations.

Through the open door policy and the intense process of getting to know the employees, you will be able to identify the existence of possible unstable situations. Again, the first steps of sharing information, negotiating expectations, clarifying roles and commitments are used to create a stable foundation. From this opportunity you can design a planned transfer or change in task assignments for the impacted employee.

You may realize that the goals of the employee and the department are not the same. The employee may be seeking higher levels of responsibility, increased opportunities to use technical skills, change in working hours, or a pay increase that you cannot provide. These conditions are discussed between you and the employee. The frustrations are settled and the employee is provided with the opportunity to accept what cannot be changed or to move on.

All of the department's remaining employees are watching you and how you handle this situation. They will see your uncompromising attitude for fairness and consistency in application of company policies. They will see a demonstrated respect for the employee and willingness to permit the employee to "save face" in this difficult situation. This first "unstable encounter" must be managed with care. In doing so your position as the manger is further enhanced.

Step 5: Making the work area and employees mistake-proof

A critical aspect of being a manager is to "protect" the employees. You can protect them from harm or professional embarrassment. With the understanding gained from the shadowing process of the complexities the employees' duties, responsibilities, and performance expectations you can take the next critical step to provide opportunities to mistake-proof your work area.

Describing Poka-Yoke methods

Shigeo Shingo introduced the concept of "Poka-Yoke" in 1961 when he was an industrial engineer at Toyota Motor Corporation.[4] Poka-Yoke literally means "mistake-proofing." It focuses on prevention and detecting mistakes and is classified as a control method that prevents possible mistakes from occurring.

> "The average American worker has fifty interruptions a day, of which seventy percent have nothing to do with work."
>
> - W. Edwards Deming

Using Poka-Yoke in everyday life

The list below illustrates how commonly Poka Yoke is used in everyday situations in the world around us:
- Bathroom sinks have a small drain near the top edge so that if the water is left running by mistake the basin will not overflow.
- File cabinets are designed so that only one drawer can be opened at a time preventing the entire cabinet from tipping over and injuring an employee.
- Fueling area on a car has three mistake proofing devices:
  - The gas cap tether keeps the cap from being lost or left behind.
  - The gas cap has a ratchet to signal proper tightness and prevents over tightening.
  - The filling pipe insert prevents larger fuel nozzles from being used.
- Automobile warning indicator lights inform you that the fuel is low, tires are underinflated, or brakes are not functioning properly.
- Electrical circuit breakers in distribution panels prevent overloads.
- Personal computers prompt you to save ongoing work and routinely to change the password.
- Automobile sensor locks the transmission shift lever in park and releases it only when you press on the brake pedal.
- Locks prevent the passenger car doors from being opened when vehicle is moving.
- Automated garage door sensors detect obstacles and will turn off the electric motor if an object is blocking the travel path of the door.
- Chain attaching a pen to the writing desk at the bank or supermarket ensures that the pen is available for the next person.

- Tools with sensors turn off the power when incorrectly handled.

Lessons from these examples in the mistake-proof world around us can be applied to your work group and department as well.

Incorporating Poka Yoke

Poka-Yoke creates mistake-proof environment through prevention, detection and incorporating solutions. As a manager, you have an opportunity to work in partnership with the employees to design procedures, policies, and processes that will prevent mistakes from being made, The goal is to quickly identify when inferior quality products are produced. Poka-Yoke *is not* an employee-training program, but rather it attacks the process and enables employees to design and install changes in procedures that prevent mistakes.

Review your notes from shadowing and make a list of the common mistakes that were identified by your employees. Work with your employees to identify opportunities and design the fail-safes, and then analyze the results of the efforts. Applaud the employees when the new systems work. The end result will be increased productivity and higher quality of work being produced. With this approach the employees will feel empowered to improve their work environment. The improving process and "mistake proofing your employees will continue.

Step 6: Writing a Code of Conduct for the Department

A **Code of Conduct** is an agreement between you and the employees. You and the work group write the **Code of Conduct**. As a work group, you all negotiate what is important in the transaction of business and in accomplishing the daily tasks. It defines the interpersonal and professional relationships of the work group. You must exemplify the **Code**; any shortcomings will be magnified.

We have provided you with a sample Code of Conduct below to use as a starting point in developing a Code, as a team effort. Notice that we said "with" the employees, you cannot dictate a Code of Conduct from the top down. Give employees an opportunity to discuss and create a Code of Conduct. There will be much greater "buy-in" if the employees write the Code. When executed properly, a Code of Conduct becomes a tool to assist employees in building positive and productive working relationships.

Reviewing a sample Code of Conduct

Below is a listing of Code of Conduct statements written by the author's department employees. The statements required time for discussion and a lot of editing. In some situations the Code can be framed and hung on the conference room wall next to the Corporate Mission and Vision statements. Another business identifies the text as "Rules of Engagement." Regardless of how you title the effort, the items below represent the values of the employees – civil discourse will prevail. The list provides a starting point to

> "I have three precious things which I hold fast and prize. The first is gentleness; the second is frugality; the third is humility, which keeps me from putting myself before others. Be gentle and you can be bold; be frugal and you can be liberal; avoid putting yourself before others and you can become a leader among men."
>
> - Lao Tzu

generate ideas for the first round of Code construction by you and the employees:

- Be on time to work, to meetings, and to other commitments.
- Be prepared with all assigned tasks completed.
- Be honest, open, and truthful.
- Be supportive and willing to assist others.
- Be informative and share critical information.
- Be willing to spend more time listening than speaking.
- Be responsible for, and openly acknowledge mistakes without providing excuses.
- Be proactive and identify critical issues.
- Be flexible without complaining.
- Be willing to give credit to others.

There are other values that can be added to the list. The important issue is that the employees create the list, adopt it as their own, post it, and then live by it in all situations within the workplace. Placing the list in a very visible location such as the staff meeting room, conference room, or in a common hallway gives public recognition that these are the values the members of your group will live by.

Providing for a dynamic instrument

The Code must be printed and displayed publicly in the work area. And, it is the standard for conducting meetings and gatherings where issues are discussed and solutions are developed. The Code, once written and adopted, becomes the instrument that sets the standard for department employees' interactions and behaviors. Over time as the work group matures you may want to revisit the Code and have the group rewrite it as a group activity. The Code remains a dynamic instrument for establishing a highly productive work environment. Take the task seriously. Do not let it be classified as a "Smile & File" task: "Smile" because the task is finished and "File" because the Code is put away, never to see the light of day again. Mount and hang the code for all to see! Give the employees the public opportunity to display with pride their work of writing the Code.

Other department managers may ask if they can copy it. The reply should be NO. The visiting manager will have to be told that the Code belongs only to members of your department. The creation process enables the employees to own the code. Without employee ownership the Code becomes meaningless and a waste of time. You can teach the manager how to create a Code but your department Code is not available to be copied.

Step 7: Selecting a Management Style

A simple, but very profound question you must ask yourself in creating a personal managerial style:

Are you the department
- *manager,*
- *supervisor,*
- *leader,*
- *servant leader,*
- *coach,*
- *mentor,*
- *guide,*
- *seeing-eye dog,*
- *disciplinarian, or*
- *prison guard?*

> "Happiness does not come from doing easy work but from the afterglow of satisfaction that comes after the achievement of a difficult task that demanded our best."
>
> -Theodore Isaac Rubin

Describing various styles

We have provided a set of definitions for the various management styles listed above. Be observant, watch other managers in the organization, monitor their behaviors and label each one using the titles we have provided. Once you have labeled the managers; observe the managers' employees and evaluate their levels of productivity, levels of mutual respect and attitudes regarding tasks at hand. You will find that the manager who exhibits or emulates the combined styles of *servant leader, coach,* and *mentor* will have the employees with the most successful levels of productivity, quality, lowest turnover levels, and highest morale.

Currently, you may have a single style, but a good manager needs to adapt several styles and be competent in turning one style off and easily transitioning to an alternate style as situations change. You should exhibit more than one style in a single day. You may identify a different managerial style not found on the list, if so add it to the list above. Try to estimate the style's value in maintaining a productive work environment.

> "A leader is best when people barely know he exists, not so good when people obey and acclaim him, worse when they despise him. But of a good leader who talks little when his work is done, his aim fulfilled, they will say: We did it ourselves."
>
> - Lao-Tzu

If you see value in a style, then practice using the style. Always look at the style's impact on the employees' morale, productivity, and their desire to solve problems. If a style does not accomplish the goal of improving the work environment and productivity then do not use it.

Illustrating the styles

Manager	A manager who plans, organizes, directs, and controls the work of others.
Supervisor	A manager who makes sure the assigned tasks are completed on time, meeting established levels of productivity and quality.
Leader	A manager who has captured the vision of the organization and shares it with others through inspiration and a display of charismatic and caring personality.
Servant-Leader	A manager who takes great care to create a work environment where all of the employees' needs to be productive are satisfied.
Coach	A manager who takes a collection of untrained and unorganized individuals and produces a winning team and earns the league championship.
Mentor	A manager who is willing to share valuable knowledge with others to ensure their success, even to the point of training a replacement. Trains employees to become successful, productive, and competent in their field
Guide	A manager who knows the path, provides the employees with points of reference to watch for, and has planned in advance for all unexpected events that may be encountered.
Seeing-Eye Dog	A manager within whom the employees place *blind* faith – who can see what the employees cannot and assures the safe arrival of the work group to a desired destination.
Disciplinarian	A manager who gives out punishment as a means of control, and does not extend

Prison Guard	rewards, recognition, and additional training when needed.
	A manager who controls and restricts the actions of all employees in the department. This approach results in creative solutions being stilled or circumvented. Creativity in problem solving or experimentation to improve the work environment are not permitted.

Assembling an eclectic management style

As a manager, you need to develop an eclectic style by choosing the best from the styles described. For some employees you may have to serve as a **Guide,** or **a *Seeing-Eye Dog***, or a **Mentor.** For others you will be **Leader** or a **Coach.** The selection of the right style for the right situation requires a lot of practice. In most cases employees will respect your use of the **Servant-Leader** style because this provides respect to the employee and also empowers them to take ownership of their own work.

New employees in training will best react to the **Mentor** role or **Coaching** approach. They will appreciate the investment of time and resources into developing their potential as a valuable part of the company. Senior employees will recognize your qualities as their **Leader** because they will be inspired by the vision you effectively communicate. However, underperforming employees will need you to be

> "We shall never know all the good that a simple smile can do."
>
> - Mother Teresa

their **Supervisor, Disciplinarian**, and **Coach** to provide focus and detailed instructions to get them through their workday.

Step 8: Producing productive staff meetings

Preparing the first meeting

Flashback to high school and the role you earned in the school play. You spent hours rehearsing with the cast members and stage crew. And, opening night arrived. The auditorium is packed. The spotlights flood the stage. You stepped out to deliver the first line. Did you crash and burn, or did you soar?

Much like that high school play performance, the first staff meeting is the chance to step out on stage in front of your employees. Will you crash and burn, or will you soar? These first few weeks of establishing managerial territory, getting to know employees, and establishing a variety of leadership styles have been complex and demanding. Now it is time to assemble employees for your first staff meeting. You are in charge; the managerial style within the meeting may include being a *Manager*, a *Supervisor*, a *Servant-Leader*, a *Visionary*, a *Coach*, and a *Guide*. But most importantly you will be a Decision-Maker.

Allow employees to voice questions, concerns, and suggestions; but the final decisions rest in your hands. Let them know that their input and contributions are valuable. You may even be pleasantly surprised by some of their ideas but, you must make the choices and decisions. There are times to be democratic, and there are times you must be a sympathetic dictator.

> "A yawn is a silent shout."
>
> - G.K. Chesterton

Each management style discussed previously has a purpose and produces a result. When combined together, the styles provide the attendees, with a manager who will create a productive meeting. The employees attending will quickly recognize that you are in charge, have a direction, and have established a purpose for the meeting. They realize that their participation will be valued and productive.

Creating meeting structure

This first staff meeting and the meetings that follow have to use the steps listed below. Here is a meeting task list to help you prepare for this critical first staff meeting and others that will follow. But always remember employee productivity is the final goal of every staff meeting.

- A printed agenda you wrote which was previously distributed to all attendees for review.
- A Code of Conduct displayed in the meeting room.
- A purpose for the meeting.
- A list of items to be discussed.
- A list of work for the attendees to accomplish and decisions to be made during the meeting.
- A list of those invited and reasons for attending.
- A precise start time and stop time.

There are four steps to execute to create a productive staff. These four steps may appear to you as being very mechanical and perhaps even a waste of time. However, the steps serve as a tool to organize and conduct the "business" of the meeting. With practice and a little planning, your staff meetings will become the highlight of the employees' workday.

Meeting Step 1: Greeting those who attend
Provide a personal greeting to each employee on arrival

to the meeting. This, of course, means you arrive early, set up the room, and you cordially welcome each employee by name to the meeting room. The room must be clean, neat, and free of clutter; all chairs are arranged, the conference table is dusted, and the room is free of debris left behind from a previous meeting. The video equipment (if used) was previously tested and is working properly. Copies of the agenda are prepared and ready for distribution.

You begin the meeting on time, to the exact minute printed on the agenda. At five minutes after the start time of the meeting the meeting room door is locked! Late arrivals are not permitted to disrupt the meeting. This may seem harsh, but employees will soon realize the value of being on time. Those who are on time will have their voices heard. Those who are late will not be late for the next meeting. They will realize the department business can and will move on without them.

> "The only way to be sure of catching a train is to miss the one before it."
>
> - G.K. Chesterton

When you extend a personal greeting to each arriving person you are providing a strong, clear message that their presence in the room is valued and you expect their undivided attention and participation. You are establishing a bond of trust, warmth, and confidence among those attending, thus creating an environment where a real productive "work group" can be formed. When this first step of recognition is missed, the need for the employees to feel accepted within the meeting is denied and their feelings of fear and distrust will be exhibited.

Meeting Step 2: Sharing information

Distribute the Agenda and discuss its content and length of the meeting. A successful meeting needs an agenda. The agenda provides the listing of topics for discussion, problems needing solutions, and decisions requiring action. Every participant must receive a copy. You organize the items by complexity and importance. The physical arrangement on the sheet of paper is important. At the top are the most complex and the most important. The amount of time allocated for each discussion item needs to be identified too. Remember the agenda provides the time when the meeting will end. This meeting ending time is a contract between you and those attending – you cannot deviate from it. If the meeting goes long, everyone in the room will stop listening to you. They will be watching the clock until you dismiss them.

In the military when the Commanding Officer calls an "all hands" meeting a very precise protocol is followed. The Admiral or General is the last person to enter the meeting room and is always the first to leave. No one regardless of importance is permitted to enter the meeting or leave early once the Commanding Officer is present. Doors are locked. At a university graduation ceremony the processional is formed with the lowest ranking students entering first followed by faculty in level of seniority, then lastly the President of the University and the commencement speaker and guest of honor. Upon the close of the ceremony the President is first to leave and the procession follows in reverse order.

In creating your meeting structure consider it as an opportunity for you to introduce simple formalities that display honor and respect. In this case you are the first to arrive and the last to leave. Here is your opportunity to build new traditions that set you and your employees apart from the run-of-the-mill department. The new traditions are important!

Informal pre-meetings with key employees may be required; you may discuss the agenda with some of the employees on a one-on-one basis to alert them and get their buy in. This is also the time to explain the locked door policy for late arrivals. This gives you a sense of how the items or tasks will be received and what the critical points are that could derail the meeting. From their suggestions, the list of items can be edited. By getting this early feedback, you have set the stage for a productive staff meeting.

The scheduling of time for each topic will require very careful thought. The pre-meetings with the key employees will do much for you in estimating the amount of time the topics will require. This second step is critical for you and the employees. Here there is a mutual sharing of the importance of the agenda, employees give their reactions, and perhaps you give them a brief opportunity to rearrange the discussion topics or remove unnecessary or "back-burner" topics from the agenda.

The employees are given the chance to share information and to help make decisions. The employees will exhibit behaviors that display openness, feedback, candor and exploration. If this important step is short-circuited, then you will quickly see the group display behaviors that exhibit polite facades and cautious strategies being quietly formulated.

Meeting Step 3: Forming goals and accomplishing work

Give the employees opportunities to set goals and do work. The employees, as individuals and as a group, need to set goals and to complete worthwhile tasks within the meeting.

Plan for and set aside time within the staff meeting for employees to work on tasks, discuss and find solutions to problems. With this successful third step the employees will manifest behaviors of satisfaction that their need to do work is satisfied and mutual growth within the work group is being achieved.

As in Step 2 above, if this activity of forming goals and accomplishing real work in the staff meeting is denied or overlooked, then you will see the employees exhibit more sophisticated negative behavior of apathy regarding the meeting. At this point, if apathy does set in, then the meeting is recognized by the employees as being pointless and a waste of their time. If this should occur, then you have a significant amount of repair work to preform to reinstate a productive meeting environment.

A successful meeting requires careful attention to even the smallest detail and the needs of the attending employees. The first three steps covered so far are the preparation for the fourth and final step in which you will see employees taking control of critical issues, forming an organizational structure through delegation of work, and producing productive outcomes.

Meeting Step 4: controlling and organizing the meeting structure

Provide the employees with opportunities to take an active part in the meeting. The meeting must give the employees time to demonstrate their skills and be recognized as valued meeting contributors. As their leader, you need to build into the list of tasks and opportunity for the employees to share in the responsibility of solving problems, accepting responsibility for work, and

> "People who produce good results feel good about themselves."
>
> - Ken Blanchard

holding themselves accountable. You need to create an environment where each participant displays the behavior of interdependence. That is, each employee is trusted by the group to be independent, yet at the same time respected by and depended upon by the group. Within this meeting environment established you now have created and achieved a state of **productivity**.

If all the above four steps are ignored in the staff meeting, then you will see the attendees sabotage the meeting, destroy any form of civil discourse, and openly declare the meeting a waste of their time by exhibiting high levels of disrespect or contempt toward you and others in the meeting. The meeting will be destroyed and employees will take it as an opportunity to degrade your credibility as their new manager.

There is much at stake here. With each succeeding meeting your skills must improve. Be patient; it takes a lot of practice, but leave no room for failure or exhibiting a casual attitude toward the meeting execution.

Meeting structure and roles for employees

Giving each person in the staff meeting a responsibility or a task to perform can enhance organizational structure within the meeting. For example, as a manager you may decide to assign the following responsibilities before the meeting and maintain the roles through future meetings.

Coaching and mentoring will be required to train the employees regarding their performance of the meeting roles. It will take time for employees to adjust to this new environment for the staff meetings that requires their active involvement. Be prepared to set aside time for employees to discuss these roles with you. Over time, the roles can be switched and changed to give each employee a variety of meeting management experiences.

Time Keeper	This person locks the door, limits the number of minutes devoted to discussing each agenda item, and sets the pace to make sure the meeting agenda items are processed in a timely fashion.
Gate Keeper	An attending employee, who keeps the conversations on topic and keeps the focus on the work to be accomplished.
Shaper	An attending employee who monitors, shapes, and consolidates key points made. This effort moves the group quickly toward a solution or decision and helps the participants recognize the best alternatives.
Note Taker	An attending employee who records the names of those attending, lists all decisions, and prepares a list of individuals who have been assigned responsibilities. This person prepares the final meeting minutes and distributes them. After the meeting, the Note Taker sends a memo to each employee listing their accountabilities and the due dates.
Coordinator	An attending employee who helps develops the agenda for the next meeting. This person works with you to ensure the right persons are invited to the meeting and the event is recorded on appointment calendars. You will have to assume this role for the first few meetings until you can find a person to fill this critical task.
Puller	An attending employee who pulls quiet attendees back into active participation thus ensuring each attendee has made a contribution. This person takes time to direct questions to those who have refrained from participating.

Supplier   An attending employee who reserves the meeting room and distributes the agenda and minutes. The Supplier makes sure other support materials and audio-visual equipment are available and operational **before** the meeting begins. This person assembles needed meeting supplies for the participants such as pens, paper, note pads, and handouts. All items are on the table and waiting for the attendees. Some meeting rooms have a coffee station – if desired, coffee, cups, and condiments should be ready before the meeting begins. The Supplier works closely with the meeting coordinator and you.

Each role in the meeting draws the employees into the business of the meeting and problem solving. The roles enable productivity to be the focal point for all involved. It will take time for the employees' roles to be implemented during the staff meetings. Be patient the long-term goal is always to make the meeting a productive event for the employees.

Producing the meeting's final product

PRODUCTIVITY IS THE GOAL and is the meeting's final product. Caution: A successful meeting comes after careful planning and practice; do not fail by failing to plan for meetings.[5]

Managing the meeting schedule

The authors found the following to be successful attributes of meetings. The employees will be watching the clock so they will be surprised when you:

Complete a 30-minute meeting in **29** minutes!

Complete a 60-minute meeting in **58** minutes!

Complete a 90-minute meeting in **87** minutes!

The word will circulate that you create positive, productive, and highly efficient staff meetings. You stay on task and do not waste their time. The most heinous offense you can commit in a staff meeting is providing employees with the feeling that it was a waste of their time.

You must quickly create an image of being a highly organized and purpose-driven taskmaster that requires active participation of all who are in attendance. The attending employees will easily see why the door is locked to late arrivals.

Maintain the **Code of Conduct** during each staff meeting.

Stay on the **agenda**.

Require the attendees to assume roles and responsibilities to make the staff meetings productive. Employees will anticipate and even look forward to the next meeting. They will come on time and prepared to participate and have their assigned tasks completed. Each will be ready to report and to be a productive participant.

Cover the **agenda**. Careful pre-planning will give adequate time for each discussion item. Do not overstock the agenda with impossible tasks. If necessary, create a small committee and give them the opportunity to find solutions outside of the meeting period. Then hold the committee responsible for the assigned tasks. The committee report is placed on the next meeting's agenda.

Restate to the employees that late arrivals will not be admitted into the meeting. The conference room door will be closed and locked; disturbances created by late-arriving employees cannot be tolerated. Late arrivals will soon change their behaviors when they realize that the staff meeting is a worthwhile event and life in the department can and will move on without them.

One of the authors, when working in the aerospace environment, was given the task of polling more than a thousand employees regarding their attitudes about regular department staff meetings. They were asked to list their concerns and the things that prevented a productive meeting. Their responses were tallied and the findings summarized. The list of their responses are provided in rank order.

Causes of meeting problems
1. No agenda.
2. No clear purpose for the meeting.
3. No defined start or stop time.
4. Wrong persons invited to the meetings.
5. No decisions made on important issues
6. Persons with decision-making authority were often not invited to the meetings.
7. Record (minutes) of the meeting's activities not maintained
8. Participants were not held accountable for tasks assigned during the meeting.

A meeting management training curriculum was designed and implemented to address each issue recorded. The skill of building an agenda was the first item within the training program!

Listing meeting action items

Productive staff meetings produce decisions and new tasks to be completed. Work will be assigned during the meeting. The employees and their accountabilities are reviewed at the end of the meeting and published in the minutes. Make sure the minutes of the meeting are distributed within 24 hours and include the names and accountabilities. Designate time during the next meeting for employees to report on work accomplished.

The staff meeting is a team meeting and you are the coach preparing for a winning season with the championship within grasp. Take each staff meeting as seriously as a winning coach does for preparing a team for the final championship playoff game. The employees soon will realize that arriving on time, solving problems, and seeking solutions is a team effort and that they will be held publicly accountable for their assigned tasks.

With "successful staff meeting" being added to your reputation do not be surprised if peers begin asking you for advice regarding meeting management. They will ask you to attend their meetings to troubleshoot. You will be asked for advice regarding troublesome employees who disrupt their meetings. You can now add another item to the list your accomplishments. In time you will be recognized as the in-house expert on creating productive and high-quality staff meetings.

A secondary result, employees will carry this attitude of creating a productive work environment from the meeting room back to their workstations. A new culture regarding work pride and, in time, active problem solving will be manifested within your group. The feeling of task urgency will be instilled. Use the meeting time to show your employees how work can be organized, tasks can be completed in a timely manner, and how being held accountable in a team environment is accomplished. This display of organizational skill will have a profound impact on all of your employees. All because you organized the meeting and locked the door!

Step 9: Writing the first set of Critical Success Factors

Defining a Critical Success Factor

A critical success factor is a daily and or weekly record of department's performance. The data are placed into an Excel spreadsheet or other database system, plotted in a graph, and publically displayed every day. With time, a trend will emerge on the graph. The charts and graphs can be introduced as a part of the staff meetings where the responsible employees will be expected to justify or explain the metrics that measure their performance.

Here are some examples of Critical Success Factors that you can measure on a periodic basis. Feel free to identify measurements that describe your department's performance. The listed measures pertain to a service business and are given only as an illustration. Experience shows that setting daily goals works the best. The actual measurements need to be recorded, charted, and publically displayed. Some generic examples of Critical Success Factors are listed below:

- The ratio of the number of customers who walk into the location and make a purchase divided by the number who simply walk in. This will provide a probability that any single customer will actually make a purchase. Over time this ratio should improve. If it declines, you as the manager need to find out why and take corrective action and hold the responsible parties accountable.
- Total sales for the day divided by the number of customers who make a purchase. This will provide the

average purchase size per paying customer. Hopefully through advertising and promotional campaigns the size of average sale will increase. If not, begin an analysis of the customers' behaviors and attitudes regarding the product or service being offered. Responsible employees need to build a plan to improve the situation.

- Total sales per day divided by the total hours worked by the sales force on the floor. This will provide the value of sales per paid hour worked by the sales force. A manager is responsible for reducing the cost of selling product at the lowest reasonable level possible. Any sudden changes need immediate examination by the responsible employees.
- Total dollars per week spent on advertising divided by total sales for the week. This calculation will provide the rate of return on advertising money spent. It also provides the impact of the introduction of a major advertising campaign. Ineffective sales campaigns will be seen easily in the numbers. Perhaps the marketing message needs to be changed, timing adjusted or other strategies investigated.
- Total delivery miles driven in a day divided by the total stops made to deliver the product. This is used to determine the average number of miles driven between stops. Over time, routes should be recalculated or redesigned in order to reduce distances driven. The goal is to improve productivity, i.e. number of deliveries per mile driven. If the average miles increase in relationship to product delivered, then immediate attention is needed by the route planners.
- Total successful deliveries (stops) divided by the total stops made on the route. This measures the potential success of any given delivery. A successful stop is defined by the customer accepting the product delivered, the delivery being complete, and stop being accomplished on

time. A measurement of satisfied customers on the delivery route is critical to business image and profitability. Changes in these numbers will require careful monitoring and corrective action.

> "Quality is everyone's responsibility."
>
> - W. Edwards Deming

- Total number of pieces rejected because of poor quality divided by the total number of pieces manufactured. This provides a measurement of waste generated or incurred within the manufacturing process. A Defect per Million Units (DPMU) is a common means of determining the level of quality. A DPMU chart on display is a critical tool in communicating to employees the impact of poor quality and the resulting waste. Use an Excel spreadsheet and equations to make this data calculation easy to perform.
- Total number of pieces created divided by total number of hours expended by the employees. This calculation provides the Pieces-Per-Hour (PPH) being generated by the work group. When plotted in a Control Chart a pattern of productivity will emerge. A drop in pieces per hour must be investigated.
- Total actual work hours divided by total paid hours will provide a percentage known as employee availability. As a manager you must hold yourself accountable for the expenditure of wages and salaries against the work force productivity. Changes in employee availability must be quickly addressed.
- Total work force availability is calculated based upon total employees and paid hours minus the hours spent away from work for personal time off, jury duty, illness, vacation, or sick time.

Explore the use of Control Charts as displayed in Quality Improvement and Control textbooks. "Is the system in or out of control?" is a critical question. A little outside reading and homework will be needed here on learning how to use Control Charts. The charts need to be displayed. This concept of a "system in control" is the foundation of the 6-Sigma theory and training.

Perhaps baselines already exist for the department. If so investigate how the baselines were calculated and adopt the standards for the work group. If not, meet with your immediate supervisor and discuss the design and implementation of a regular data collection and recording process. As the data are collected and displayed, you will be able to evaluate your group's performance.

Writing the Critical Success Factors

REMEMBER THE TIME YOU spent shadowing employees during the first week? Now is the time to revisit the notes and identify areas for periodic measurement where performance data can be extracted. Various activities need to be measured daily and or weekly. The elements to measure are the frequency of the activities, the cost of the activities, the profit of the activities, or the time consumed to complete the activities.

The goal is to change systems that will enable you to complete the activities faster and cheaper, while improving quality and meeting the customer demands for the service or product. This may appear to be an impossible set of goals. However, if

> "Profit in business comes from repeat customers, customers that boast about your product or service, and that bring friends with them."
>
> - W. Edwards Deming

each activity is studied in detail, critical success factors or metrics can be designed, data are collected on a periodic basis, and graphs and charts are created. From the observation and identification of patterns, new approaches and changes can be made.[6]

Within the work area, you need to display these charts that are updated daily or weekly. Each chart shows the productivity of your department and the employees. Special due dates, or better known as "drop-dead" dates, are included and displayed, listing the tasks that must be finished and who is responsible. They serve as the thermometer that measures the performance of the department. Visual performance displays on the wall are an excellent method to communicate expectations to the employees.

You will have to reserve space on the corporate computer server to save the Excel spreadsheets that contain the departmental performance data. The data should never be stored in an employee's desktop computer files. All historical data will be lost with a hard drive crashes, a computer is stolen, or by a disgruntled employee who likes to delete the files. This data are far too valuable to allow such casual storage or maintenance. Your performance and your employees will be documented in the database. Treat the database with care! Make backup copies; assume the worse will happen and take all steps required to preserve the database from all possible negative situations. Over time the files become a historical record that tracks your efforts as a manager.

Teaching employees to measure their own efforts

Do not overload employees with the production of manually prepared performance reports. If possible have the reports prepared automatically by the corporate computer. Meetings with Information Technology staff will be needed to obtain custom reports. While compiling the reports repeatedly ask, "What is the value of this information?" and "How can I use it to improve my department's performance?" If you are not going to use the data, then do not waste time in gathering and analyzing the information.

Create a list of possible performance reports. Ask staff members to review the report list; annotate them with comments. Once a core of critical success factors are identified reports can be generated. After trend lines and Control Charts are produced, the employees will weave the information into their daily activities.

STEP 10: DISCOVERING AND EVALUATING GROUP'S INFORMAL LEADERS

Discovering why informal leaders exist

Within your department there are employees that are qualified to run the daily business, perhaps even better than you. Why are they not in leadership? The answer is quite simple really, management is imperfect and some people are not good at ensuring that the supervisor knows that they are doing a good job. Some informal leaders fear the responsibility of leadership but instead feel comfortable directing from the sidelines.

Employees evaluate everything you say and do. Others in the group will turn to the informal leader for guidance in confusing matters. Some may perceive that your guidance and decision making is lacking. When goals of a large project are ill defined, when performance standards are not clear-cut, or when the number of people assigned to complete a task has not been provided, then the employees will fill the vacuum with their own information. They will turn to someone i.e. informal leader who can answer their questions.

> "Never forget that only dead fish swim with the stream."
>
> - Malcolm Muggeridge

Informal leaders will challenge your authority; if they do, then politely, firmly put them in their place. Words are best. Think carefully before acting. In some environments, you may have to defend yourself with persuasive leadership skills. If you sense you are being pushed, push back immediately and harder. Even if you perceive what you are doing is correct, change it a bit. Change times, allowances; cost ratios, whatever you can to stake out your territory.

If you do not push back, the informal leader will keep taking territory until you eventually will have to confront that employee. This will be a messy conflict, where you may lose. Upper management is judging you by how well you handle each situation. You must step up and fulfill the duties as leader; if you step out of the leadership character, you will lose control.

Remember, do not try to be a friend to an employee; in the end, they will despise you for doing so. You may be friendly, but not a friend. They have friends, and they want you to be their leader. Military officers act like officers, and military enlisted personnel act like enlisted personnel. The informal leader will create a complex situation for you. The first step is to recognize that the informal leader does exist in your department.

Describing an informal leader

Employees in the work group give power and authority to the informal leader through a quiet display of recognition and respect. The informal leader is the person to whom other employees can:

- Turn to when a special resource is needed and normal channels do not work – *dispenser of favors.*
- Rely on for providing answers to questions – *guardian of privileged information.*
- Depend upon to communicate needs up the chain of command – *possess inside links to higher levels of informal leadership.*
- Depend on to display disrespectful or disruptive behaviors – *possessor of secret information and a confrontational attitude.*
- Seek to step in and publically invalidate or countermand your decisions – *possessor of the organization's oral traditions and history of previous failed solutions.*
- Provide an inside approach to completing normal work day assignments – *knows the minimal effort required to produce the minimum quality and still get through the day.*
- Run to when facing disciplinary action for unacceptable behavior – *knows the small loopholes in organization policies and regulations.*

The informal leadership within the team is an influential force that you have to reckon with. The actions of the informal leader will have a profound impact on all new hires that you bring into the work group. The new hires will want to assimilate into the group as quickly as possible. The new employee may be directed by employees in the department to the informal leader. You must deal directly with the informal leader and the influence on the new employees.

The complexity of the informal leader's impact in the work group can be identified through observation. New employees receive three types of training:

The first is the employee orientation delivered by the HR Training Department.

The second is the effort to give the new employee on-the-job training that provides the technical skills needed to be a productive member of the work group.

The third is the training received from the informal leader. Here the new employee is taught the work group's secret survival techniques: what your soft spots are and how you can be manipulated, intimidated, or pushed into a corner.

It may take a while to recognize the messages being communicated to the new employee by the informal leader. Just be aware that informal survival training does exist in all organizations and at all levels. Ignoring this fact will not make it go away. Informal leadership is an interesting phenomenon that has to be firmly dwelt with by you, the new manager.

Ferreting out and neutralizing the informal leader's impacts

The informal leader will not be easy to see, but with time you will begin to perceive the real impact the informal leader has on you and the productivity of the employees. The following is a list of observations to help you understand the impact of the informal leader:

- Measure the employees' reactions to the public display of productivity metrics.
- Examine the culture of the work group.
- Review the work history of each employee including promotions and disciplinary actions.
- Acquire a list of the previous "hard" decisions made by other supervisors, how the employees reacted, and the final outcomes.
- Explore the history of department employee turnover rates and reasons for employees leaving.
- Conduct confidential interviews with all recently hired

employees requesting open and honest appraisal of the working conditions.

Watching employees' behaviors and how they solve the workday problems is a good place to start. It will help you discover who holds the informal power position within the department.

Understanding the informal leader's goals and attitudes

Below is a sampling of possible goals of an informal leader:
- Maintaining a position of power and authority over employees you are supposed to be managing.
- Controlling resource allocation to employees in the group.
- Providing disruptive behaviors at strategic points in time to degrade the outcomes of your decisions and to affirm that the informal control continues to exist.
- Creating situations that weaken your leadership and authority.
- Satisfying a personal need for the feeling of power over you and others.

Getting the informal leader to acknowledge department leadership

As the incoming manager or supervisor, you have only one choice. The informal leader's unproductive behaviors have to be controlled. You must gain control, get on top of the situation and stay there. This section deals with how to handle the informal leader.

Develop a plan with the support and guidance from the HR Department that is designed to correct the behavior or terminate. This activity can be a slow and painful process. However, the employees who are seeking open and honest leadership will

> "The key to being a good manager is keeping the people who hate me away from those who are still undecided."
>
> - Casey Stengel

soon recognize that you desire to improve the integrity and productivity of the entire work group. They may be resistant to the efforts at first, but once they see that you are doing these things for the good of the group, they will come to respect your decisions and actions.

Termination will often prove to be the best solution, and the action has to be accomplished if you are to keep the leadership position. You must carefully review the HR policies and be sure to follow them precisely. Maintain an accurate documentation of the informal leader's performance. A case can be developed that leads to termination or transferring the informal leader to another department. It is imperative that you dot the I's and cross the T's in this process. If you intend to create a case for terminating the informal leader of the work group, you must follow company policy exactly to avoid the risk of firing the employee unlawfully. If you are not careful, you could lose the respect of the employees at best, or face litigation at worst.

Transferring is a possible solution. However, such a transfer will have to be carefully coordinated with the receiving manager and the HR Department. If you cannot break the hold of the informal leadership and HR will not let you terminate, then the only choice may be to abdicate your position, resign, and seek employment elsewhere.

This is a battle of survival: the old way continues or you take the management position and carry out the responsibility for which you were hired. Old processes are built upon the need to perpetuate the individual informal leader's survival.

The survival and improved productivity of the group, however, is the desired goal. This is accomplished through teamwork, sharing of multiple responsibilities, cross training, job sharing, and taking full responsibility when errors are made. This is a difficult set of concepts to absorb, but once ingrained within the group then productivity and job security will improve and the informal leader will become powerless. Again, the actions of the group's informal leader cannot be pushed aside.

Measuring Performance as a Manager

CHECKING FIRST MONTH OF PERFORMANCE

Within the first month on the job, you should set up a meeting with your immediate supervisor. Do not be surprised if the supervisor or manager is unprepared and feels awkward regarding the request to talk about the first thirty days' performance. You may have to take charge of the meeting. Explain that you want an informal first-month performance review. Keep a small notebook handy; the supervisor will probably start out with either praise or criticism, finishing with the other. Take notes and quietly set personal goals for future performance and levels of expected productivity.

You will find that the supervisor may not know what

> "Leadership, like swimming, cannot be learned by reading about it."
>
> - Henry Mintzberg

you are thinking and may assume the worst. However, with an open and honest dialogue, much will be gained for the both of you in this early stage of being the new manager.

Present a list of all that you have accomplished. A good place to start the conversation is with the Critical Success Factors and the display of the improvements in the metrics. It is likely that word has gotten back to your supervisor regarding the efforts you have expended to date. Review the goals you have set for the employees and correlate them with the corporate vision and mission statements and the improvements recorded against the Critical Success Factors. After comments have been noted, request another follow up meeting to continue the conversations.

Measuring the Critical Success Factors

Always seek to communicate what you are doing on a regular basis. Try to schedule periodic meetings for mutual feedback and critique of your short-term department goals. The topic of the meetings should be the Critical Success Factor metrics. Each measurement when displayed as a trend over time or control chart will graphically display your ability to manage the department. A set of possible questions to ask yourself when preparing for the meeting:

- Have the measurements of the trends of employee productivity, quality of product produced, response time, and or employee morale shown improvement?
- Have the operating expenses and operating budgets displayed the outcome of implemented cost controls?
- Have the programs that are designed to bring the department's Critical Success Factors into alignment with organizational expectations been successful?
- Have the projections regarding future performance

exhibited a reasonable slope (improvement) that indicates progress is being made?
- Have you attempted to assess employee morale and what steps have you taken to improve the employees' attitudes, productivity, and perceptions of the department?
- Have a list of action items that address the Critical Success Factors been developed?

With time and experience, you will develop more sophisticated Critical Success Factor and Control Chart measurements and projections. It is important that you archive the periodic measurements (databases) on the corporate computer server for use in future studies.

Again, do not be surprised if other managers come to visit with you and request guidance regarding the development of their own performance metrics. A valuable support skill to master is the use of Microsoft Excel© for data analysis and plotting trends. If you do not know how to use Excel©, then Go online and take a quick course or find a book and teach yourself.

As a manager you need to be able to analyze data quickly and competently. Do not hesitate to add this computer skill to your toolbox! A very simple quote from W. Edward Deming and Peter Drucker illustrates this discussion: ***"You can't manage what you can't measure."***

Checking what should have happened and creating a repair list

From the performance meeting create a list of what the supervisor wants to take place, what you need to improve, and what are the levels of expected performance. Involve the supervisor in the development of the procedures to ensure that you are doing what management wants you to do. However, with each "opportunity for improvement," create a possible solution for the situation.

This is the "hurt list" wherever you have fallen short, things that you have to fix. Apologize to those you have affected by your mistakes, accept corrective instruction, and get the repairs done. Make note of where the mistakes were made and how they occurred. From this analysis, be on the alert to recognize a possible similar scenario, and then take steps to prevent a repeat. Mistakes will occur but to continue making the same mistakes more than once will produce a terminal effect on your career.

Building a "shock absorber" attitude between the employees, the supervisor, and the customers

No one cares about your feelings; neither your supervisor, nor the employees or the customers. If they want you to have feelings, they will give you some of theirs and often they do. All three groups are clamoring for attention. Give them the attention they desire, but remain the adult. Be respectful to your supervisor, subordinate to the customers and superior to the employees. In some situations, you may be the only adult in the room, so be the parent in a polite way.

When a difficult situation or conflict occurs in which you must apply the full effect of being a shock absorber, plod through the event keeping full control of feelings and the situation. Make note of the cause. Was it a breakdown of existing policy or procedure, a failure of the performance of an employee, or a "perfect storm" of unforeseen and uncontrollable

> "A real leader faces the music, even when he doesn't like the tune."
>
> - Anonymous

events? How you handle the situation will forever be remembered by the employees. Did you first seek to openly blame others, create a story to cover yourself, or accuse the wrong employees? This event will be one of the defining moments for you as a new manager. Plan the responses and to repair the damage very carefully.

We suggest the following actions be taken:
- Record notes of the situation and its cause. Identify key players, the applicable policies and procedures, and how each played a part.
- Formulate a corrective action plan.
- Take the steps necessary to rewrite a problematic policy or procedure as needed.
- Implement the revision in the training curriculum if it appears new employees are being incorrectly trained.
- Introduce the need for changes or revisions during the next regular staff meeting without identification of those involved.
- Close the matter as it will not be publically discussed again.
- Monitor the environment to determine if the changes are effective.

The workday continues and you provide the image of being untouched, stable, and totally in control. The goal is always to improve the quality of the work environment and employees' productivity. Those very close to you will know of the emotional stress you have endured. The employees must never know. There is no room for revenge and vindictive comments or behaviors. This is the shock absorber attitude that is so very difficult to master and implement. It goes against the very nature of your emotional being, but is vital to the professional success as a manager.

Planning for next year's performance review

The informal review of your performance with your supervisor at the end of the first month sets the stage for the future first annual formal evaluation of your efforts as a manager. At the one-year mark, there should not be any surprises. The weekly or monthly meetings with your supervisor addressing department metrics, established goals, and the employees' performance will be a good indicator of the review outcome.

The author of this text, as an undergraduate and graduate student, took the time during each semester to visit with each of his professors. The question he posed to the professor, "What do I have to do to earn an A in your course?" Most of the professors were taken back by the question, were unprepared, and needed a few minutes to formulate an answer.

> "Be a yardstick of quality. Some people aren't used to an environment where excellence is expected."
>
> - Steve Jobs

The mystery and the secrecy of their grading systems (which were quite possibly arbitrary and capricious) had to be lifted. Now it became a discussion of performance and of the quality of work expected. Each professor took time to respond and their grading criteria were discussed, work was identified, and course expectations were summarized. With the performance list of work in hand, a plan was created by the author for each course to complete the assigned work, master the concepts, improve analytical thinking skills, plus do a little extra. At the end of the semester, after implementing these strategic plans, an A was awarded.

This approach continued to be used after graduation in every position of employment. The common thread that reappeared in every conversation was the degree to which the professors and later the supervisors were unprepared to provide a set of precise performance metrics. To earn the "exceeds expectation" or the academic "A" rating, you have to know the scale and the expectation. Do not be surprised if you supervisor cannot provide a concrete answer. You will probably have to step up and write the performance criteria for yourself.

Take charge of the conversation with the supervisor, use the Critical Success Factors and present the plan and metrics to earn the superior performance rating. At this point you are developing a standard that probably would exceed anything your supervisor could have conceived. This fact will further impress the supervisor and will create a great deal of job security for you. Quietly enjoy the moment!

Setting up the accountability meeting with the supervisor

The first priority is to provide your supervisor with commitment, support, and loyalty. In addition, rally the employees and set the direction for the future productivity of the work group. Your supervisor must see you often and hear from you how the team is doing. If you do not speak to the team regularly, someone else will move in on you and start reporting on you. It might even be one of the direct reports. Go to lunch with your supervisor or manager, talk on the phone and meet in person. Keep your supervisor informed regarding work group's productivity. Use the supervisor's open door management style and visit.

CHECKING THE FIRST SIX MONTHS AND MEASURING THE CRITICAL SUCCESS FACTORS

When you have been in the managerial position for six months, evaluate your performance as if your supervisor was evaluating you. Use the job description, trends from the Critical Success

Factors and Control Charts metrics, employee feedback during the Open Door meetings, work accomplished in weekly staff meetings, and the goals adopted in earlier meetings as a starting point. Take the time to review your performance and what you have contributed to the organization. List what is now running better, how improvements have been adopted, and what are the projections for the second half of the year. With the homework completed, you will be ready for the six-month performance discussion. Take personal pride in what you have accomplished and let a little bit of that pride show during the meeting.

Earlier, Critical Success Factors and their purpose and design were discussed. Six-months have quickly come and gone. You have created a productive work group and you have measured their individual performances. During the past six months you should have, daily and weekly, recorded performance as a manager and as an employee who submits to your supervisor. Each Factor's measurement becomes a score to compare against a pre-established set of goals.

For the runner, the ultimate goal is to break the 4-minute mile barrier. For the golfer, it is to play a par golf game on every course. For the baseball player, it is pitching a perfect game. This six-month period provides you the opportunity to gain an honest and very personal review regarding your performance. With an honest personal perspective, you will be ready for a conversation with your supervisor regarding the benefits and improvements you have brought to the department and to the organization.

Getting ready for the first formal performance appraisal

You represent yourself, goals for the work group, and the performance of every employee under your command. Therefore, to prepare for the appraisal of the accomplished work requires you to do introspective analysis in each of these categories. You should rely on personal diaries, meeting notes, filed e-mails, and data collected relating to your Critical Success Factors. Of course, your supervisor conducts the meeting and the direction of the meeting will be determined by the supervisor's attitudes, perceptions, and analysis of skills displayed as a manager.

> "Far better is it to dare mighty things, to win glorious triumphs, even though checkered by failure... than to rank with those poor spirits who neither enjoy nor suffer much, because they live in a gray twilight that knows not victory nor defeat."
>
> - Theodore Roosevelt

From this analysis of your own performance you need to bring to the meeting a new (upgraded) set of performance standards, a plan to address the shortcomings, and a list of professional development opportunities.

Establishing goals and accountabilities for the employees

The most critical element of your performance review is to produce the next set of performance standards for you and your department. You and your supervisor have to write the new set of accountabilities. This is a serious matter. Over the years, the authors have interviewed professionals who report they had never had an open and honest performance appraisal. Some report of never having had an appraisal in a face-to-face meeting. One of the quiet fears of any manager is having to evaluate the performance of another. This performance documentation, once committed to writing, leaves a feeling of vulnerability for the one who does the evaluating. Thus, it is often easier to avoid the appraisal than to take the final step of completing the evaluation. This is why managers may not give or receive performance evaluations.

When you have a performance review with your supervisor, you have the opportunity to build a professional relationship and set meaningful goals for yourself and the work group. Do not be afraid to negotiate goals and expectations. Every member of your work group will be "watching" and "listening" to see what the outcome of your meeting will be. The result of this performance review sets the tone for the work environment for the year to come. With a successful performance review your work group and your leadership are affirmed.

CHECKING THE FIRST YEAR OF PERFORMANCE

As you approach the end of the first year, the following metrics as described at the earlier portions of this book will provide insights regarding your managerial performance. The following measurements should be considered:

- **Your Performance Goals and Critical Success Factors:** Have you achieved the goals that you set for yourself and those set by your manager? The graphs that plot the daily and weekly Critical Success Factors are the measurements that display the goals that have been accomplished.
- **Your Employees' Productivity and Performance Goals:** During the meetings with your employees, you will have established their productivity goals. Were the goals met? Were they realistic? Did you and the employees voluntarily reset and establish even higher sets of standards for performance?
- **Your Employees' Attitudes and Work Environment:** Do the employees' attitudes reflect positively toward you, toward their daily assignments, and toward their desire to work as a team? Attitudes are perceptions that are not quantifiable but you have

to depend upon your skills in "reading" the employees. Some indicators are their willingness to participate in casual conversations with you, jump in and voluntarily take on extra work, come to work early to prepare for a special task, or research opportunities to improve the quality of their department's work.

- **Your Employees Attendance and Turnover Rates:** How stable have the employees been during the first year? Employees' performances are measured in their availability to be on the job, be at their workstations, and be productive throughout the day.
- **Your Department's Contribution to Organization's Profitability:** How have the employees been actively involved, as a team, in improving the quality, productivity, and profitability of the department? Which, in turn, resulted in the improvement of the performance of the company? This is an ideal example of your leadership skills and ability to consolidate employees into a high performing team. In other words, did your team go all the way and "earn the championship"? Did your department set the example for other departments to follow? Do other managers turn to you and seek advice?

Setting performance goals for the first year

Critical Success Factors supplied by your organization or those that you have created for yourself provide the tools to accomplish the measurement of the performance of the group. These factors produce information in different categories that build databases that contain measurements regarding product quality, work group productivity, employee attendance, and individual productivity. From these measurements, you are in a position to respectfully negotiate performance standards. Within the organization, standards may be set without room for negotiation. You will want to exceed those quality standards, especially by improving employee morale and the resulting productivity.

Each rating is measured in mathematical values; such a goal is usually set in percentage or numerical values. With thought and careful analysis, you are ready to set a new standard of performance for the next twelve months and present them to your supervisor. At this point you have made a commitment to your work group, and to the organization that your efforts will be measured, and will be directed to achieving these goals.

Department goals are published for all to see and regular posting of ongoing metrics show how achievements of the goals are taking place. The employees will be able to watch the changes take place. In one organization the author works for, large flat panel television screens are mounted and the metrics, graphs and charts are fed to the screen using a computer and are updated continually throughout the day. All employees can see the positive as well as negative changes occurring within their work groups.

Your professional development goals should focus on personal growth and improvement as a manager; listed some goals for reference:

- Attend training courses in conflict management, project management, human resources labor law, project management, writing performance reviews, or introduction to accounting or managerial finance.
- Take specialized training for skill-building in Microsoft Word©, Excel©, PowerPoint©, Project©, or Access©.
- Read a book that provides the theories and mathematics that are the foundation for Continuous Quality Improvement.
- Work toward earning the Lean Six Sigma Green and Black Belts.
- Join a professional society or organization that supports

the practice of management and organizational development.
- Learn a new language.
- Create an informal group of fellow managers and meet regularly to share ideas regarding the practice of management. Read and discuss a popular management text. Present unique problems for group analysis and solution building.
- Subscribe to and read regularly a business journal such as *Quality Progress*.

Rating the first year by looking in the rear-view mirror

Now it is time to rate your performance in preparation for the first year review. How would you write the commentary regarding the past year? Using the measurements in the prior section:

- Would you say that you and the department (team) had a good season?
- As the coming year or new season begins, what are the possible plans to improve the team's performance?
- Do you need to make new assignments or move employees to different responsibilities?
- Do you need to begin new training, updating, or replacing of the tools to work with? Bring in new employees or transfer employees out of the department?

> "In the business world, the rearview mirror is always clearer than the windshield."
>
> - Warren Buffett

From the analysis, you are ready to construct the strategies to take you and the team through this coming year. Are you going to build upon the past year's experiences or just simply repeat the first year over again? This is a true test of your managerial skills and ability to grow and achieve a higher set of goals for the department. There are managers who simply keep repeating the first year's mistakes over and over again. You have the opportunity to use the first year's experiences, build on this foundation, and prepare for a second year of exciting new set of accomplishments.

Repeating the first year again or starting a new second year

The planning for the second year begins with the review of the goals you set for the first year. Did you create a set of goals for this first year that are classified as being SMART? As Paul J Meyer said, "Attitude is everything."

Were the goals **SMART?**[7]

S – Specific - Significant, Stretching, Simple
Goals must be very precise and describe the situation very carefully. Vague terms or jargon have to be avoided.

M – Meaningful - Motivational, Manageable, Measurable
Goals must have criteria that can be easily recognized using standard data collection and measuring techniques. Progress toward accomplishing the goal can be tracked.

A – Attainable - Appropriate, Achievable, Agreed, Assignable, Actionable, Adjustable, Ambitious, Aligned, Aspirational, Acceptable, Action-focused
Goals have to address tasks that can be accomplished using the current available resources.

R – Relevant Result-based, Results-oriented, Resourced, Resonant, Realistic
Goals that are specific, measurable, and attainable are classified as being relevant. All of the employees involved

in the goals will acknowledge that the goals pass the test for being reasonable.

T – Timely Time-oriented, Time-framed, Timed, Time-based, Time-bound, Time-Specific, Timetabled, Time limited, Trackable, Tangible
Goals need a completion date, a predetermined point in time when the effort will be accomplished. Some goals may involve a set of individual activities that, when accomplished, create a finished effort.

This is a scorecard to measure the effectiveness of the first year and set the standard for the second year. You committed yourself to making the first year a success. Staff meetings were organized, goals set, a team trained, and interpersonal skills enhanced. Only you can honestly appraise how effective the efforts have been and then estimate what the future holds for the second year. The following checklist may guide the introspective process:

1. Measuring the accomplishments and number of goals completed

You are in the position to determine the degree of success in accomplishing the goals for the first year. Was the effort reasonable? Did you earn the respect of the employees? Do the employees see the efforts as being of value? Did accomplishing the goals improve employee morale, productivity, and quality of work? *Was the effort you invested in accomplishing the goals worth it?*

2. Reviewing the Critical Success Factors and the supporting databases

The **Critical Success Factors** you created allowed a daily and weekly measurement of the performance of your work group. Did the posting of the critical success factors improve the employees' awareness of the work group's performance? Did the success factors show a steady improvement during the year? Were the employees actively engaged in the data collection and analysis? Did the employees' behaviors change for the better? Do you see their change in behaviors as an indication of your leadership skills?

3. Examining the individual performance review reports of each employee

The employees' performance reviews and goals they set for the next year offer a snapshot of the employees that form your work group. If all of their goals were placed into a single list, what work would they accomplish next year? What percentage of your employees are rated as just average performers? In your estimation which of these employees will improve their performances the next year? A very difficult question now follows: ***Do you see potential in investing a second year of time in serving as the employees' leader?***

4. Checking the degree of employees' turnover and fluctuations in morale

Employee turnover is a measurement of your hiring and managing skills. Were the right persons hired? What were the reasons for employees leaving? How effective was the recruiting process? Do you wish that the employees who have remained with you would actually leave? ***What happened to the best employees? Did they stay and support you or did they move on to bigger and better opportunities? Or did they become discouraged and voluntarily leave?***

These questions, if handled honestly, will give you an indication of the future you face during the year to come.

Each of these four evaluations will give insight regarding your managerial and leadership skills. This listing, if taken seriously, provides you a starting point to plan the coming second year.

Keeping the supervisor on track and managing the supervisor

It is important to realize that the standards of performance that you have set are real, and your supervisor expects you and the work group to perform. Do not be too exacting or ambitious in your goals. Your supervisor reports to someone else – make sure you understand that relationship. If something goes wrong, the blame may be placed on you. Be alert to your supervisor's mannerisms and behavior; with practice you will be able to read them.

If you are good at your job, you may find that the supervisor feels threatened. This is a difficult situation; little can be done to fix it. However, remember you can always quit the company or move to a different department. The key to being successful in management is to always look for ways to make your supervisor look good. Provide an uncompromising attitude toward achieving the Critical Success Factors. All decisions must be based on the highest level of ethical standards, integrity, and honesty.

Evaluating the Organization, Division, Section, or Department — A Better Place Because of the Year You Invested

The following questions provide you with additional food-for-thought.

Evaluating performance from a historical perspective

- What is the previous history of your managerial position?

- What was the reason for creating your department and how long has it been in existence?
- What managers preceded you within the department?
- What was the length of time the previous managers serve in your position?
- What were the employee turnover rates for the previous managers?
- What is the "word-in-the-halls" or reputation regarding the department, the employees, and the previous managers?
- What are the general opinions of the other managers regarding the department? Do you think these opinions are accurate?
- What significant unsolved problems did the previous managers leave for you to solve? Have you solved the problems?
- What was the style of the previous manager: a managerial giant, an incompetent fool, a progressive explorer, or an absolute dictator? What lingering impacts did these perceptions have on you and your group?

The first year for you and the battles you have had to fight were governed by the questions above. In a very honest self-appraisal, how do you answer each question above? Did you investigate each question before taking this management position? How would you rate yourself? With the evaluation, only you can derive a final opinion of your performance.

Adding Skills and Capabilities as a Manager

Coaching employee performance

A high school coach serves as a perfect illustration. At the beginning of a sports season the coach begins the process of organizing the players, and assessing their skill levels and their desire to play. During practice hours, the coach continues to run the drills, hone skills, and build a team. At the first game, the coach appraises the performance of the team and each player. The next week's practice brings more skill building and teamwork exercises. The coach uses discipline, praise, recognition, repositioning members on the team, constructing new plays or strategies, and setting goals to build a winning season.

Your players or employees began the season with you as

> "Always do your best. What you plant now, you will harvest later."
>
> - Og Mandino

an unorganized, undisciplined, and unskilled group. Your task as a coach or manager is to build a winning season with the employees you were given. However, the actual composition of the team, the employees' positions on the team, and the game strategies are left to you the coach and manager. You as the manager inherited this team, but you have the opportunity to build the new team, create the first-string, refine the employees' skills, and assign responsibilities. You, the coach, receive the credit for building a winning team; the players-employees receive the credit for performing as champions. Are you willing to accept the opportunity to build a winning team and earn the division title? Does the team look forward to a winning season? Can you take this team to the playoffs?

Managing using diagnostic skills

Recognizing symptoms and prescribing treatment for a diseased organization

The approach of a manager viewing an underperforming, disjointed, or chaotic work group as diseased was introduced to the author by Vic Downing, President and CEO of Global Advantage, Inc. as derived from his training of business leaders within international organizations. The view of a group as being healthy or diseased provides the manager with a perspective to design a treatment plan for returning the group to a healthy state.

> "Management is doing things right; leadership is doing the right things."
>
> - Peter F. Drucker

A medical doctor has a predetermined definition of a healthy person. Measurements are taken during a physical exam – height and weight, temperature, blood pressure, blood chemistry, reflex systems, eyesight, teeth, bone structure, and joint flexibility. When complex symptoms are present, then tests that are more complex are required. As test results come in, the medical doctor assembles a treatment plan to restore health. The plan may span the spectrum from a simple medical prescription to the more extreme of surgery, transplants, reconstruction of bones, muscles, or organs, weeks or months of therapy and medications.

A highly skilled repair technician has a definition of a properly running automobile. The fuel system, braking system, electrical system, and power transfer system all have normal expectations and ranges of operation. The technician will begin the diagnostic process with the established operational standards in mind. Makes and models all have different levels of expectations, but regardless of the ranges the engineering performance requirement standards do exist. The quality of performance is measured. As the technician makes repairs and replaces parts, the new level of performance is compared against the established performance standard.

Defining a healthy organization

A skilled manager must know the characteristics of a healthy organization. You, as a skilled manager, need to have predetermined performance standards for your work group, department, section, or division. This set of performance standards creates the opportunity for you, like a doctor or auto technician, to measure the existing condition or health of the employees' and the organization's performance. A manager has the opportunity to fix and repair (prescribe a treatment to heal) the work group, but that can only happen if you have a definition of a healthy organization.

Fixing or changing an organization without a goal or purpose cannot be justified in any situation. Such attempts to create change within an organization without a goal in mind which has been thoroughly communicated to and understood by the members of your organization will create distrust and suspicion among the employees. In time, your creditability as a manager will be eroded and eventually destroyed.

Planning to heal a diseased organization

In the section above, the concept of a Critical Success Factor needs to be brought into this organizational analysis and discussion process. With the human body, the measures range from a simple blood pressure metric to the analysis of nerve impulses within the brain. You, as the manager, will need simple measures to get a snapshot of performance, such as absenteeism percentage, daily output of work, quality of product produced, number of complaints from internal or external customers, and the passive-aggressive behaviors of employees who attempt to sabotage productivity or production schedules. As you write the definition of a healthy organization follow the steps listed below:

Step 1: Gathering information

Collect the Corporate Management and the Human Resources Department Standards. Such examples of standards would be:
- Budgeted expenditures by department.
- Budgeted annual sales or other performance goals.
- Product quality standards.
- Product delivery standards.
- Number of days employees are permitted to be absent without an excuse or being a "no-call-no-show."
- Number of days permitted for "leave of absence."

- Copies of job descriptions for each employee you are responsible for.
- Copy of the corporate mission statement or objectives.
- Copy of the annual CEO's State of the Organization letter or speech.

Step 2: Organizing information

Carefully examine all expected standards and create a list that will be convenient to use. Identify the ones that specifically relate to the work group and move them to the top of the list. Part of this analysis process will require you to develop a set of normal production standards for each operation that is performed. The average and acceptable rates of performance are now available for you to compare to current and future performance. The standards must be published and available to all employees. The employees need to understand from where the standards were drawn and why they exist.

It is time for you to make the comparison between observed and measured behaviors and the accepted performance standards. You are now ready to begin the role as a diagnostician and create a plan to heal your work group. With the application of a proper "treatment" plan the work group can be cured and the chaotic and unproductive performance removed.

> "Someone's sitting in the shade today because someone planted a tree a long time ago."
>
> - Warren Buffett

Step 3: Identifying the problem or disease

With the acceptable standard and actual performance metrics available, you will be able to determine the degree of difference and the complexity of the disease that requires immediate attention. Now, it is time to find the root cause of the difficulty.

The process of sorting out possible causes is subdivided into four areas. Every organizational problem is traced back to one or more of the 4-M's: **Manpower**, **Material**, **Machine**, or **Method**.[8] The diagnostic process requires the analysis of the work environment from these four perspectives.

Manpower (Employees)

Sample of things that could tie the employees to the problem-disease:
- Insufficient levels of training or nonexistent applicable skills that pertain to the task.
- Lack of required physical strength or endurance.
- Work hours scheduling do not meet the product peak demand requirements.
- Members of the work group are not a match for the task.
- Sabotage of production as a symptom of employee dissatisfaction.
- Grievances are left unattended and the number of accusations continue to increase.
- Low morale and or bad attitudes, continuing personal conflicts, lack skills to settle disputes.

Material

Sample of things that could tie materials to the cause of the problem-disease:
- Input material does not meet acceptable quality standards.
- Stock supplies are not sufficient to maintain steady production.
- Source suppliers cannot guarantee just-in-time deliveries.
- Shelf life of raw materials does not meet production standards.

> "The best executive is the one who has sense enough to pick good men to do what he wants done, and self-restraint to keep from meddling with them while they do it."
>
> -Theodore Roosevelt

- Excessive handling produces material damages.
- Storage practices lead to damages.
- Inventory systems do not accurately record storage locations for needed product.
- A change in product suppliers has produced deficiencies in acquired product quality.

Method

Sample of things that could tie employee work habits to the cause of the problem-disease:
- Assembly process requires steps that employees are unable to fulfill or is inefficient and steps could be eliminated to improve productivity.
- Quality control checkpoints do not provide timely or adequate feedback.
- Large supplies of sub-assemblies that cannot be improved once defects are detected.
- New standards have been established for final product but assembly methods have not been adjusted.
- Availability of sub-assemblies for production runs are not properly timed.
- Large quantities of waste are generated when assembling the final product.

Machine

Sample of things that could tie hardware to the cause of the problem-disease:
- Operations are out of calibration and do not remain in calibration when adjusted.

- Production cannot meet capacity requirements.
- Spare parts for machines are not readily available.
- Planned maintenance cycles for equipment do not fit within the production run requirements.
- Machines are out of date and new technology is needed.

Step 4: Troubleshooting and problem identification

Classify the issues identified by the four categories listed above. Rank the symptoms by level of impact on the problem at hand. Solving the problem may require a multiple of treatments.

<u>Category</u>	<u>Treatment</u>
Manpower	employee training, conflict resolution, employee attendance records evaluation, team building, morale building, work environment conditions improvement, improving leadership effectiveness and credibility
Material	purchasing for quality standards, Standard Operating Procedures (SOPs) evaluation and rewriting quality control practices
Method	employee training, hand-motion study evaluation, charting of production methods, productivity evaluation
Machine	engineering studies of machine operations, technician calibration procedures, timely repairs, acquisition of spare parts

From this analysis, you have completed the preparatory steps of building a treatment plan to return the diseased work group's state of health to normal. The analysis and treatment plan development requires a combination of skills to include (1) people skills, (2) engineering skills, (3) production planning skills, and (4) the earned respect of the employees who need to trust you to fix the problem-disease.

Training the employees to recognize an organizational disease and then produce their own treatment plan

Once you publicly post the productivity standards and the work group's actual metrics, and you have completed the 4-M evaluation, you are now ready to begin the process of implementing the treatment plan. You use a managerial style and serve as a "guide dog" when taking the employees through this disease identification and treatment plan process. They will see each step, from recognition of the problem to the final stage of observing the corrected operation. Collect and post metrics so the employees can watch the change take place. The work group observes the final results: higher productivity and improved quality of delivered product.

In preparation for the second cycle of problem identification, create a focus group and give the employees the opportunity identify a problem, collect the symptom data, perform the analysis and design a solution (treatment plan). As you create the opportunity for the employees to build self-confidence, take pride in their work environment, and want to take responsibility for improving productivity, they will become diagnosticians and will carry on the effort.

CONDUCTING PERFORMANCE REVIEW MEETINGS WITH THE EMPLOYEES

Performance review meetings are the most important ones that you will have with the employees, and

> "All anyone asks for is a chance to work with pride."
>
> - W. Edwards Deming

you will probably have some stress regarding the task. No one likes the meetings, neither the manager nor the employee. Yet, the task of evaluation must not be delayed, get the first round completed as required by the HR Dept. Consult with the HR Department regarding the corporate policies governing employees' performance review schedules, meetings, and timing.

Below are some preparatory steps you need to assemble for the first employee performance meeting;

Performance evaluation forms as supplied by the HR Dept.
- Performance evaluations from the previous year with notes and any employee signed statements.
- Job description to be used during the meeting.
- HR Handbook or Guidelines for conducting employee performance review meetings.
- Meeting agenda and calendar are coordinated with HR Department.
- Meeting time and place is arranged. Select a time and place that permits an uninterrupted atmosphere, which is private, and away from the work group. Calls and messages must to be rerouted or delayed to prevent any interruptions.
- Agenda is created that sets the topics for discussion and the length of the performance meeting.
- List of the employee's Critical Success Factors or previously established goals that were to be accomplished as established by you or the previous manager. The documentation of the degree of effort expended relating to each goal.
- Documentation of employee's work history, dates of hire, pay adjustments, promotions, awards, transfers, daily productivity or quotas, daily attendance records, and training history have been acquired and copies made for the employee. Include list of outstanding

accomplishments. What were the employee's "above and beyond" efforts?
- Personal notes you have made during Open Door meetings and while visiting with the employee.
- First draft of performance goals you have written for the employee to review and discuss for the next year. It is important that the employee feels there is a partnership and cooperative spirit in adopting the new set of goals.

Designing an employee performance review meeting

The meeting's content, and sequence of discussion topics requires careful thought oriented toward what you as the evaluator desires as the meeting outcome. The following discussion may shed some light on the reasons performance review meetings are feared by both the manager and the employee.

Point of note: The authors have polled hundreds of employees and supervisors regarding expected outcomes for performance review meetings and have listed them here for your consideration.

Anticipating the two different points of view

The supervisor expects that the employee:
- Will show a respectful demeanor with an appropriate level of humility.
- Will recognize and accept without question the established goals and performance standards that have been established by the company.
- Will not raise provocative questions or issues or attempt to derail the meeting with an argumentative attitude or disruptive behaviors.
- Will quietly accept the criticism or judgment to be pronounced by the manager.
- Will maintain a dignified composure.

- Will leave the meeting quietly and acknowledging the wise judgments provided.
- Will eagerly look forward to performing all of the newly assigned tasks.

The employee expects that the supervisor:
- Will provide honesty and commitment.
- Will show sincerity in all issues.
- Will provide recognition and praise for work accomplished.
- Will acknowledge awareness and sympathy of the organizational-induced difficulties that prevented the employee from realizing a full potential.
- Will set aside time discuss how to train to improve performance.
- Will give career counseling to identify current and future promotional opportunities.
- Will show interest in discussing the employee's career goals.
- Opportunity to expand professional goals.
- Reinforcement of a team effort.[9,10]

The two sets of impressions provided above illustrate the dramatic differences in points of view of the employee and supervisor that can occur within the meeting. Thus it follows that confrontation and conflict is highly possible and probable during the supervisor-employee performance review meeting. You must consider the employee's point-of-view and build into the meeting the opportunity for open and sincere dialogue between the two of you. Your demonstration of personal self-confidence in actions of and the respect toward the employee is the secret to creating a positive outcome for the performance review meeting.

The company controls the environment of an employee.

If the employee is critical of the company's lack of support, the employee is usually correct. Do not automatically mistrust the employee. The majority of employees want to do a good job; sometimes the managers feel like the employee does not. This is your

> "A stiff apology is a second insult... The injured party does not want to be compensated because he has been wronged; he wants to be healed because he has been hurt."
>
> - G.K. Chesterton

opportunity as the new manager within the performance review meeting to reverse negative attitudes and create trusting and lasting positive working relationship with each employee. It is the authors' belief that employees are not inherently lazy, only confused or overworked, which are the byproducts of poor leadership.

Recognizing conflict within the work group

Understanding why conflict exists

Conflicts come into being when an image of **opportunity** is faced along with the possibility of **danger**. For example, the **opportunity** for a company to grow and expand is a desirable future. However, such growth requires investment of capital and related debt to the lender or the investor. The **danger** is always lurking – increased revenue from the growth may not be realized and the debt may not be paid. The planning for such a venture creates opportunity for conflict as sides are taken. The **growth** point-of-view sees the **opportunity** of establishing a dominating position in the market place. The

non-growth point-of-view sees the uncertain future and the predicted increase in revenue as being unrealistic. The **danger** of the company's potential destruction is real. Conflict quickly emerges and when resolved, the careers of those on the losing side can be in jeopardy.

You, as a strong manager, must weigh both sides, seek to reconcile, and create a strategy that will lead to the best solution. Paths that minimize the maximum regret outcome and maximize the positive opportunity must be sought.

Seeing opportunity vs. danger

As a manager, you can become the generator of conflict. As an example, you see an **opportunity** to improve the employees' productivity. You have spent hours evaluating the current systems and procedures, and you can easily see the opportunity to change and create an improved process. The opportunity appears to you as such a simple thing. The employees see the **danger**; they may mistrust your intentions. Will you give them increased pay for doing more work? Will they be able to learn the new skills and methods quickly enough? Take the time to step outside the emotions of the situation and develop a strategy to take control and produce a constructive and positive outcome.

> "It takes 20 years to build a reputation and five minutes to ruin it. If you think about that, you'll do things differently."
>
> - Warren Buffett

The simple secret is for you as the manager to evaluate all of the possible perceptions of conflict from the employees' point-of-view. Look at the **opportunities** and **dangers**. As conflict emerges between employees or between you and the employees

– invest the time in quiet analysis of all of the opportunities and dangers. There will always be the chance that the dangers will outweigh the opportunities; the opposition may in fact be correct, and you have a false impression of the benefits.

The most difficult situation to face as a manager is the possibility of having to back down in the conflict environment. This will take a lot of inner strength but the result will be the betterment of the whole work group. If the employees have seen your trust in them then they, in turn, should manifest trust in you. You need the personal inner strength to acknowledge that your analysis may be in error. Your employees will recognize the situation and their respect for you will increase because you are willing to admit an error in judgment.

The discussion below identifies the stages of conflict and how to recognize them. The table was the product of professional graduate students participating in a MBA course taught by the author on the subject of conflict management in the workplace. The text assigned for the course appeared lacking regarding the topic of recognition of conflict stages. The students were challenged by the author to outperform the text and build a matrix of their own, as shown below. Several other classes of students contributed to the effort. Over time and after a series of refinements the chart was created.[11]

Recognizing the various levels of conflict

Level 1: Personal internal feelings

Symptoms: Employee has a small internal feeling. A nagging uncertainty is kept from the view of others.

Treatment: Open door management will encourage employees to share their thoughts and feelings privately. Concern can be dissipated and/or refocused by the manager.

Level 2: Casual conversations

***Symptoms*:** Internal feelings of concerned are shared with another person. The conversation is informative and troubling feelings are revealed.

***Treatment*:** Stay in constant contact with all employees. Staff meetings offer an opportunity for open and honest sharing of ideas. The issues can be brought into focus and correct information shared.

Level 3: Animated conversations, others involved

***Symptoms*:** Positions are formed, discussions emerge, and positions defined are as facts are brought into the exchange. Raised voice levels are used to establish points of view.

Treatment: A sensitive and well-trained manager recognizes that passion brings out strong feelings. Meet privately with those who represent the opposing points of view. Give them the responsibility to work together as a team and reconcile the expressed differences. Seek for solutions that will be implemented immediately.

Level 4: Sides are chosen

***Symptoms*:** Others are drawn into the discourse. Points of view are clarified and the numbers of persons involved increases. Opposing points of view and individuals are aligned. Points of view are polarized.

***Treatment*:** The strong feelings have to be faced. The structure of the work environment can seriously be impaired. Distribute accurate information. Opposing point of view is recognized and a plan to reconcile is put into place. The conflict cannot be allowed to escalate.

Level 5: Specialized tactics adopted

***Symptoms*:** The opposing points of view begin using special tactics to include name-calling, insults, threats, verbal attacks, and publishing of false information to establish a position of dominance.

Treatment: Remove the employees from the work environment and place them on administrative leave. Bring in a neutral mediator. Establish a strong leadership; distribute correct information. Implement strong corrective actions and penalties for destructive behaviors. Employees are given notice of termination if situation is not controlled.

Level 6: Win at all costs

Symptoms: One point of view clearly must lose. The line has been drawn; one side must win. Possibility of the destruction of employees' health, welfare, safety, and careers become part of the win-lose environment.

Treatment: Third party mediation is mandatory. Remove employees from the work place. Both sides' points of view are recognized and very strong intervention program is implemented. Members of both parties must submit their resignations if negotiations are not successful and destructive behaviors by members of the group continue.

In the early stages of conflict, you need to give the employees the tools to constructively deal with differences of opinions or perceptions. You must be able to quickly appraise the stage of the conflict and immediately confront the situation. Lack of leadership on your part in the face of accelerating conflict will destroy your creditability as a strong manager and possibly even destroy your career. Review the chart above carefully and recognize the level of conflict and then apply the appropriate intervention. It is critical to fit the appropriate remedy to the level of conflict.

Keeping support staff supportive

You need to take the time and make the effort to earn the respect of the support staff. Support staff – who are behind the scenes such as CAD CAM engineers, inventory clerks, copy machine repair, vehicle repair, custodial staff, and IT maintenance staff – create the work environment that enables you to succeed. The employees' productivity is directly tied to the support team's cooperative attitude. Create a support staff focus group that has the responsibility to report to you regarding opportunities to improve their productivity. Invite a representative from the support team to the weekly staff meetings. The following suggestions will provide recognition of their hard work:

Building relationships with support staff

In dealing with support staff, make a point of meeting with the leader of the support staff and be introduced to the group. If they accomplish a difficult task for you, send an accolade to their leader with a copy to your supervisor or better yet meet with each support person. If the support department asks for a report that is difficult for you to assemble and to provide, then ask for guidance in how to complete the report. Do not argue with the requestor about whether the report is important; they do not have control over the report. On the positive side, the department will instruct you in how to navigate the situation if you politely ask for help.

Giving support staff an opportunity to contribute to the team environment

Do not hesitate to ask for help from the various departments; human resources, budgeting, engineering, information technology, and facilities. You may find them standoffish at first, but if you are politely persistent, they will give you the magic solutions to the problems. Why are the employees standoffish? Because they probably have been ignored, insulted, and or underappreciated by previous managers. Your job is to correct that and show the support staff how valuable they are to the organization.

> "A person without a sense of humor is like a wagon without springs. It's jolted by every pebble on the road."
>
> - Henry Ward Beecher

FINDING HUMOR IN THE WORKPLACE

As a manager, you need to be able to recognize the various types of humor and develop strategies to use humor in the work area. There are two basic types of humor, constructive and destructive. Constructive humor, when properly used, is a method to relieve stress, make light of difficult situations, and develop common bonds between employees. On the other hand, destructive humor insults, belittles, and devalues the actions of others. Destructive humor is the foundation for building a hostile work environment.

- Some forms of destructive humor may lead to legal action and very costly outcomes. A wise manager uses constructive humor to build opportunities to reduce stress, put complex activities into perspective, and create an enjoyable workday. Employees must be given opportunities to express positive humor and be trained in the dangers of destructive humor. Humor is a vital element of a positive productive work area. Humor is a powerful force and tool when used by a skillful manager.

PREPARING THE EMPLOYEES FOR BIGGER AND BETTER OPPORTUNITIES

Things to think about:

It is interesting that within the educational systems, beginning on the first day of the school year the principal, counselors, teachers, coaches, security personnel, and support staff spend all of their effort preparing the students to successfully complete the year and to eventually graduate and leave the campus for other opportunities. The school staff are motivated by the idea that students who do dropout, fail to graduate, or who must repeat the same grade twice produce a negative mark against the school and the school staff. Thus, it is in the school's best interest to produce students who are successful and leave the campus when training is finished.

In the medical care industry, all efforts by the doctors, specialists, nurses, and technicians are for the patient to be healed and leave their care as quickly as possible. From the medical perspective, the goal is to produce a healthy productive patient in a minimum amount of time. Concerns are raised and, at times, legal issues come to bear when a patient is slow to heal and or remains too long within the recovery process.

Helping the employees build careers

As the supervisor and leader, you have the responsibility to provide the employees with the opportunity to build their careers and for each to move up and beyond the department's work environment. This prospect may cause discomfort for you. Critical questions should come to mind:

- Why would you want to spend time replacing employees who leave the work group?

- Do you have the time to train newly hired employees only to watch them leave?
- What is the benefit to you, as a manager, to spend the effort required to replace good employees?
- What will your manager think when your best employees leave the work group?
- How do you reconcile the fact that your employees will eventually grow up and out of their roles?
- What happens when the employees develop skill levels that are beyond those required for the completion of their daily department tasks?
- Do you encourage employees to earn college credit or degrees, which will eventually create dissatisfaction with their status quo as team members?
- Will you provide the employee with time away from work to seek additional training or education?
- Do you network with fellow managers and offer them opportunities to recruit your best employees?
- Are you willing to help an employee write a good resume and assist the employee in improving their interviewing skills?
- Do you pass along to the employees the news or announcements of job opportunities outside your department?
- Do you refer the best employee to other managers who are looking for workers who can help them turn around a disorganized work group?

These are all very uncomfortable questions for you to face as a manager. One of the authors of this text worked in aerospace for a company that had 100,000+ employees worldwide. The workgroup managed by the author consisted of fifteen engineers with graduate degrees in the sciences. The group produced cost estimates for changes in various strategic weapons systems for the military. A newly hired employee within the cost estimating department would take about eighteen months to become competent in the cost-engineering process. After the challenge of learning the how-to-produce-cost-estimates, the task quickly turned into repetitive and less than challenging exercises for the employees.

Producing superior performers developing employees who will leave

While interviewing new candidates, a negotiation process was included by this author; that is, an honest discussion was opened between the author and the prospective employee during the interview. The potential nature of the task was explained and the commitment was made to assist the employee upon being hired in the move-up-and-out process. Thus upon hiring a partnership was formed between the supervisor and the new employee based upon an open and honest dialogue regarding job expectations and possible future opportunities.

> "Too many leaders act as if the sheep... their people... are there for the benefit of the shepherd, not that the shepherd has responsibility for the sheep."
>
> - Ken Blanchard

In this aerospace cost-estimating department, it was okay for the employee to master the task and eventually become bored. It was okay for the manager to help the employee find more challenging opportunities. The end result was a highly motivated group of employees who were committed to the tasks at hand and who valued an ethical work environment based upon mutual trust. Some of the employees selected to move on; others felt comfortable and remained within the department. The clear message was that to move on was acceptable and could be planned for. The partnership between the manager and the employee was based upon an open and honest exchange.

Friendships were also developed among the department employees. Over the years reunions are held; former employees share the new events in their lives. Email newsletters keep all posted. Those memories working together as a team will never be forgotten.

Hiring new employees

Finding the right employee, or just filling the spot for now and hoping for the best

You as the manager will often be faced with a shortage of employees, major deadlines are looming over you, and your supervisor wants the work finished yesterday. As manager budgets have to be maintained with funds allocated for salaries and wages. Thus, an opening can create two types of pressure: one, the work is not getting done; and two, the budget dedicated to paying the open position can be removed. Therefore the pressure you face to get the work done and to consume the budget allocations for salary produces a lot of stress. Sometimes the ideal applicant cannot be found and the fallback position is to staff with a second-choice candidate. You as as the manager must design programs to bring this new

> "We hire people who want to make the best things in the world."
>
> - Steve Jobs

employee up to speed. Inferior performance cannot be accepted.

Employee turnover results from the following:
- Employees are terminated because they violate company policies and or procedures. This can never be negotiated. A strong and firm approach in such a situation will earn you the respect of the employees. The employees already know who has to leave well before you will. The productive employees, those who want to be part of a successful department, will support such an action of termination.
- Employees are offered positions in other departments, divisions or organizations. They are seeking new challenges or opportunities and give you advance notice and, if given the chance, can help select a replacement.
- Employees are transferred to an alternate position within the organization, and such decisions regarding movements are often out of your control. Staying in touch with fellow managers is the best way to be informed of such pending decisions.
- Employees are seeking retirement or wish to take an extended leave of absence for medical or personal reasons. These employees are helpful in identifying and interviewing internal and external candidates based on their knowledge and experience.

When a position is vacated, you have opportunities to fill the opening. The first is to search within the immediate division for employees who may be interested in joining the department. Making the announcement through the HR Department and professional networks is the best approach. HR posts the announcement and job description on the organization's website. The second is to have HR advertise to the outside labor market and seek out applicants beyond the bounds of the organization.

Interviewing process

Once you have a list of applicants, the next step is to filter them and select the "best of the bunch." In addition, with the selection you have three different approaches to pick the final applicant:

- **Single interviewer** This is a one-on-one meeting. You or a designee will meet with the candidate, discuss qualifications, and seek to understand how the person will contribute to the organization. Is there a match between the applicant's job skills and the job requirements? A direct comparison is made between their answers and the task requirements.
- **Interview panel** This is a small group of employees who have been trained in appropriate Interview protocol. The panel should be composed of employees and supervisors who currently perform the tasks the applicant is expected to perform. Once the interviews are completed, the panel will discuss the interview results. The panel then ranks the applicants and submits the names to the person who will make the offer.
- **Interview panel and assessment center** This requires each applicant be given a series of tasks to perform that typify day-to-day work. Such an approach requires a lot of advanced planning and coordination with the legal representative in the HR Department. An assessment center provides simulated tasks and skills required of the position. The interview panel participates and evaluates the products the candidates produce. A ranked list of applicants is created and submitted.

Thus, you have created an opportunity to select the best candidate the labor market can produce.

New employee welcome and orientation:
- A good start creates the best opportunity for an employee to be successful. Typically, the new hire receives an HR and Payroll orientation regarding company policies and procedures. An identification badge is printed and, if needed, protective gear or clothing is issued. Benefits are explained and enrollment forms are completed. Once the orientation steps are completed in the HR Department, the new employee is escorted to your department.
- Select a senior employee within your department to work next to the new employee to answer questions and provide guidance. A side note: make sure that you reward that senior employee in some way periodically to avoid a situation where the old employee sabotages the new. You want this senior employee to know that the extra work you are assigning is valuable and the efforts are appreciated.
- Use the following questions to review the new employee orientation and training program:
    - Have you observed the new employee orientation program?
    - Does the orientation provide the needed information regarding company policies, benefits, and payroll?
    - How does the technical on-the-job training take place and who is responsible?
    - Will the employee receive specialized training and or equipment certification?
    - What training will you personally provide to the new employee?
    - How will you introduce the employee to the members of the department?

- What are you going to do to make sure the new employee's first assignment is completed on time and with a level of quality that meets the department's standards?

Hiring a new employee is a very costly, tedious, time-consuming and at times awkward experience for the applicant, and the rest of the department. The measurement of your managerial skills is based upon the quality of the new employees you bring into the department. The hiring of new employees is an excellent indicator of your managerial skills. Take this effort very seriously; there is much at stake, and it must not be treated as a casual experience.

> "There are basically two types of people. People who accomplish things, and people who claim to have accomplished things. The first group is less crowded."
>
> - Mark Twain

Letting employees go

- As the new manager you may be faced with the task of "cleaning house." Business as usual (following past bad practices) and employees' behaviors may be unacceptable to you and to upper management. The previous manager, whom you are replacing, may have had a reduced standard for performance, reduced ethical standards, a blind eye to corporate policies, or extended favors to gain favor. Whatever the reason for letting someone go, most are reluctant to terminate an employee.

Taking disciplinary steps

The procedure to manage disciplinary actions with an employee requires a precise strategy. Generally, a series of steps will lead to termination. In some cases immediate termination can occur when the employee is involved in actions as intolerable behaviors such as falsifying hours worked, endangering the safety of other employees, theft of company property, or possession of controlled substances. However, companies differ; talk with your supervisor and the HR Department before any action is taken.

The following steps identify the process of dealing with an employee whose actions do not comply with the established standards:

Step 1 – First Occurrence

Identify the corporate policy or procedure that was violated; obtain the name of the employee, and the degree to which the activity disrupted the company standards, and provide an example of the correct behavior to the employee. Obtain names of witnesses.

Meet with your supervisor and a representative from the HR Department to review the company policies regarding the use of disciplinary action. A documentation of the event is prepared and discussed with employee. The employee's signature is obtained. This is usually called a "training corrective action" or a "plan to improve performance." The goal is to inform the employee of the correct procedure or process so that the error will not be repeated. Next, a time limit is established to improve the level of performance.

Step 2 – Second Occurrence

Set up a meeting in a private location away from the normal flow of work. Have a meeting with the employee in the presence of an HR representative. Within the documentation, clearly identify the violation, and provide an example of the correct behavior to the employee. Provide a copy of the page from the employee handbook or manual. Describe the next action that will be taken if the violation occurs a second time. In some organizations the third event will result in termination and others it is the fourth event that produces termination. *Provide copies of the documentation to the employee and for the HR personnel file.*

The goal is to have this occurrence be the last. The follow-up training, monitoring of behavior, and praise by the supervisor for completing the task correctly is usually sufficient and no further disciplinary action will be needed.

Step 3 – Third Occurrence

Document this occurrence in writing. Have the third meeting with the employee in the presence of an HR representative. During this meeting, the employee is informed of this second violation and told that this event or the third will result in termination. Check with HR to make sure the sequence to termination is correct. The employee, you, and the HR representative sign the documentation. Provide copies of the documentation to the employee and to the HR Department for placement in the employee's personnel file. Additional training is provided.

The goal is to have this occurrence be the last. The follow-up training, monitoring of behavior and praise by the supervisor for completing the task correctly may be sufficient and no further disciplinary action will be needed.

Step 4 – Termination

The third occurrence results in termination, as specified in the previous occurrence documentation. Set a time and place for the meeting with the employee and the HR representative. Notify your supervisor that you plan to terminate the employee. Meet with HR representative to review the documentation to receive their approval for termination. HR and Payroll will prepare the final paycheck and the letter of termination.

Terminating procedures

If you have completed all of the steps above, and it is necessary to terminate the worker's employment, the following procedures should be followed:

- Arrange for an HR Department representative and company security personnel to attend the meeting. The employee is informed of the termination. You then leave the room, and the Human Resources person finishes the transaction.
- At the meeting the security person takes the employee's badge, building keys, and other property belonging to the company. The guard escorts the employee out of the building and off of the premises. The employee is not permitted to return to the work area or talk with any of the employees on the way out.
- The security personnel will clean out the employee's desk, files, and or locker. All personal property are packaged and mailed to the employee.
- The termination cannot be discussed with other employees for any reason. The privacy of the terminated employee must be protected. Fellow employees will have a lot of questions but you cannot discuss any aspects of the situation. If you should see the terminated person later, absolutely do not discuss the matter. Be cordial and polite, but do not bring up the termination.

Controlling unemployment benefits

The opportunity for the terminated employee to receive unemployment benefits needs to be addressed here. As a manager, you and the HR Department have the responsibility to make sure the employee has been properly terminated, following the carefully established company procedure and employment law. By doing so, the terminated employee cannot successfully file legal action against the company for an unjust termination, or be successful in obtaining unemployment insurance payments.

However, the termed employee will file for unemployment benefits. A court hearing will be scheduled and the HR representative will be responsible to show the hearing officer that the termination was properly managed and the employee was given opportunities to correct behavior. If the hearing officer determines the employee was improperly terminated, documentation was lacking, and the opportunity for corrective behavior was not provided – then the unemployment benefits will be awarded to the employee.

> "It's just that, when the orchestra looks at me, I want them to see a completely involved person who reflects what we rehearsed, and whose function is to make it possible for them to do it."
>
> - James Levine

When such an event occurs, the company will have to face increased unemployment insurance fees. Unemployment insurance is much like auto insurance; every time a driver is involved in an accident the insurance rates increase. Likewise, every time an employee is improperly terminated, benefits have to be paid and the organization's unemployment fees are increased. An improper termination of an employee then results in an increase in the operating expense for the company.

Your responsibility and HR's responsibility to carry out the termination correctly cannot be understated. Make sure that you follow the company policy carefully; do the research well ahead of time. The HR Department must be the partner and take the lead role in this employee termination process.

MANAGING A PROCESS AND A PROJECT

You as a manager will be given the opportunity to manage processes and/or projects. There is a significant difference in the managerial skills required to be successful in each. They are not the same; a process and a project are very different. The following discussion points out the differences:

Defining Process Management

A **Process** is an ongoing repetitive activity performed by a group of employees. A **Process Manager** is responsible for the generation of process work on a regular basis. In a large sense, there is little variation in the tasks or work output. The process manager must maintain a stable and competent work force, and produce a quality product that meets the customers' needs. Listed below are examples of work faced by a process manager:

The process manager must be able to understand and plan a workflow and be able to answer the following questions without advanced warning or notice:
- How productive is each employee?
- How much time is consumed by each employee's task?
- How long do employees remain in the work group?
- How do employees complete the tasks as described within their job descriptions?

- How are the department's productivity records and budgets kept current and accurate?
- How are you using the department reports to optimize employee productivity and reduce the operating expenses?

Below is a list of knowledge and skills required of a process manager:
- Know the external and internal customers.
- Know the customer requirements.
- Know each employee's skill set.
- Know how department budgets are maintained.
- Know how to maintain a steady work output regardless of employee vacation or leave time requirements.
- Know how to anticipate the need for expanding or reducing the size of the work group.
- Know how to estimate the need for new hires and then have the training program ready to be implemented.
- Know the inter-relationships between tasks that define the daily flow of work.

Examples of processes are provided below to illustrate the activities a process manager would oversee:
- Review applications for permits, waivers, and licenses.
- Generate daily, weekly, and monthly productivity reports; financial reports; employee turnover data.
- Complete sales to customers.
- Receive customer complaints.
- Organize groups of people.
- Create products to be distributed to customers.
- Repair broken machinery.

Defining Project Management

A **Project** is an activity performed by a group of employees that has a start date and a finish date, a budget for constructing the project, and a set of design standards. In a large sense, the project uses specialized skills and resources only for the life of the project. The project manager must have a goal orientation, be technically competent in the field, and be able to assemble a team of employees for a short duration (the life of the project).

Examples of projects

- Move a division of employees to a new building or location.
- Sell a portion of the corporate holdings.
- Hire new group of employees who have a specific set of skills.
- Upgrade a computer system to include new hardware and software.
- Rewrite and adopt a new Standard Operating Procedure (SOP).
- Purchase support equipment for a new training program.
- Remodel a building.
- Assemble a design team to create a set of plans (specifications) for a new building or system.
- Design and implement a new public relations program.
- Create a research and development team to design a new product line.

As a **Project Manager** you must be able to answer all of the following questions regarding the project without any advanced warning or notice:

- How much have you spent so far on the project and will you remain on or under budget?
- How long will each project activity take and will the completed project meet the delivery deadline?

- How do the people you are hiring provide the necessary skills to bring the project to completion?
- How is the project filing system designed and is it easily accessible by all members of the team?
- How are the project records and budgets maintained?
- How do you deploy the correct number of employees with appropriate skills?
- How do you use the project planning tools such as the PERT and Gantt charts to anticipate future problems?
- How to anticipate the inter-relationships between project tasks and activities?
- How do you estimate the timing of the interconnected activities that will produce the final project?
- How does the project work schedule identify project milestones and project reviews dates?
- How will you bring the final project effort within cost (budget), on schedule and within quality/performance specifications?

> "The key to successful leadership today is influence, not authority."
>
> - Ken Blanchard

A measure of your project management ability is to have answers for the questions listed above.

Project Charter

The first step of being a project manager and accepting responsibility for the project is to write and negotiate a **Project Charter.** The **Project Charter** contains:
- The description of the project and all technical specifications.
- The budget and schedule of activities.
- A listing of employees and skill level requirements.

- The final project tests and evaluations for the completed project.
- The project manager's authority to control expenditures, schedule activities, sign contracts, and allocate employee tasks.

This **Project Charter** has to be negotiated and signed by all parties before the project begins. Once it is signed, you as the project manager may begin the project.

Project Manager: One who is technically competent and has earned respect

Others will judge your leadership competence, based upon your technical expertise. **Project Manager** is a high-risk position for you, for your supervisor and the organization. If you fail, everyone related to the project fails. Consequently, only when you have earned the respect of your colleagues and are rated as technically competent are you ready to be considered for the role of a **Project Manager**.

Project Manager: Decision-making authority

In the project charter, your decision-making authority must be clearly defined. For example, the following list of responsibilities requires definition within the charter:

To whom do you as the project manager report?

An organizational chart will show to whom you report and show your relationship to the other process managers who provide employees to be members of the project team.

If you are reporting **too low** within the organizational structure, then you must realize that the project has very little importance to the organization. This condition will create significant decision-making problems for you throughout the life of the project. The beginning of the project is the time to establish proper reporting levels and you should attempt to do so.

If you report **too high** in the organization, then your fellow managers may become antagonistic toward you and uncooperative when you request for loan of employees to work on the project team. The way to counter this is to have individual meetings with peers to enlist their cooperation as equals. If they sense that you are going to lord it over them, by using them as stepping-stones for your success, you have failed before you started.

If you report to the person in charge of initiating the project and who manages the supervisors you will be turning to obtain the project team members, then you will have the political power to carry out the project.

Do you have hiring and employee selection authority?

Do you have the authority to pick and choose the employees from various process departments for the project team?

If you report too low in the organization structure then the process managers will *give* you their most **unproductive** employees to be members of the team. Your negotiation and "earned respect" tools will be needed here to obtain the best possible employees for the project team. By this time, you should be known as someone who shares the credit for successes. In that way, although you will be increasing the workload of the process managers, they know that they will be receiving accolades as teammates. Make sure they attend the final meeting when the project is declared finished and that you praise them for their support of you and the project.

With technical competence, earned respect, and the charter

in place you have the authority to pick the best employees for the project team.

Do you have budgeting and expenditure of funds authority?

Do you have the authority to create and maintain a separate set of accounts and can you generate purchase orders with your signature for the project?

Without a budget and spending authorization, you cannot control the progress of the project. Working relationships and agreements must be established with the finance department well before the project begins so that payroll, purchases, and budget reviews run smoothly. Invite a person from the finance department to the project planning meetings; they will smooth the path. This forethought and accommodation must be carefully written into the project charter.

Do you have project-planning support?

Do you have project management support software (Microsoft Project©) and persons dedicated to maintaining accurate records that can withstand unannounced audits for the project?

Without project management software to provide control over budgets, activity scheduling, and progress reports, the project is doomed from a budgetary and a political standpoint. The highest degree of accountability must be maintained – there is no substitute for accurate and complete recordkeeping, even if you have to do it yourself. However, it is best to have a support person to provide for data entry, provide weekly reports, and attend project management and reporting meetings.

How often will you have project review meetings and project milestones?

Do you have a project schedule (Gantt Chart) in place with project milestones identified?

The Microsoft Project© software package will serve as the foundation for all information management. Microsoft Project© software provides a valuable tool for the project manager to track project progress. Several books are available and explain how to use Microsoft Project to produce timelines, budgets, schedules, and task assignments.

Without continuous and systematic public accountability review of the project progress the project will be doomed to failure and your career damaged or destroyed. The project charter must identify to whom you will report the progress of the project. Here the project activity schedule, budget, expenditures to date, manpower performance, technical problems and solutions are discussed in detail.

> "Meetings are a great trap. Soon you find yourself trying to get agreement and then the people who disagree come to think they have a right to be persuaded. However, they are indispensable when you don't want to do anything."
>
> - John Kenneth Galbraith

Agenda for project planning and management meetings

The project meetings have a special function and purpose. The meetings provide a status check on the progress of moving toward the project's completion. The frequency of the meetings you hold depends upon the size and complexity of the project.

Generally, meetings are held weekly. Monday mornings represents a good time to review the progress made during the past week and review activities planned for the week ahead.

All members of the team must be present at each meeting to report the progress on their activities. Ensure that HR, Finance, and other supportive departments have someone in attendance as well. Make a point of being early and greeting each person as they arrive. Provide an agenda and refreshments, if you can afford it, and enhance the standard company fare. Use the first section of this text regarding meeting management as a guide.

Find out from the office meeting organizer what refreshments are normal; some companies do coffee and donuts, others serve Danishes and orange juice. Learn how to make coffee, if they use it, even if you do not drink it. A no-coffee situation for habitual coffee drinkers is a brutal situation; if you live through one, do not allow it to happen again. On the Friday before the Monday morning project meeting, informally poll the project team members for feedback about the project, this gives you the weekend to formulate an approach and assembling the agenda for the next project meeting.

Project activity planning and budgeting meetings

The following is a list of agenda items for the weekly project meetings:
- Analysis of each activity's planned start and actual completion date.
- Review of project schedule milestones – both completed and for the future.
- Review of slippage of due dates and justification for date variances provided by project team members who are responsible for the individual activities.

  Do not be confrontational, once a problem is identified, ask the identifier for a solution in a friendly manner. Make sure that you pause long enough for the project team member to think and to respond. This moment will be an opportunity for a project assassin to respond and make others look bad. Criticism and support comments must be informative and non-confrontational.

- Review of the project's Gantt charting of activities optimistic, expected and pessimistic completion dates. A project management textbook will be very helpful here.
- Review of the project's Project Evaluation Review Technique and Critical Path network.
- Analysis of project budget and all planned expenditures vs. actual expenditures (those over and under budget).
- Review of all expenditures' variances with justification provided by project team members.
- Critical issues affecting the project's successful completion are identified and documented. Responsibilities and accountabilities are assigned.
- Project team member performances are summarized.
- Corrections (if any) to project schedules and budgets are listed and documented.

This list of agenda items is repeated every week until the project is completed. From this list you can see that employee' integrity, honesty, and willingness to own up to errors are of paramount importance. You as a project manager must seek out these strengths in the employees you invite to the team.

Matrix management in the project environment

A **Matrix** management environment requires employees to report to two or more supervisors. The employee could be working in the accounting department (a process), writing the monthly auditor reports and at the same time, the employee would be assigned to a project team that is designing a new computer local area network. The accounting department manager expects the process employee to produce the reports in a timely manner. The project manager expects the project team member employee to attend all project meetings and provide meaningful input and solutions to problems. A matrix environment produces tremendous stress as the employee who must serve two masters for the time as part of the project team. Maintaining a productive matrix work environment will test all of your management skills to the maximum. The rewards will make the extra investment of effort worthwhile.

Since the project is often a temporary task with a short stress period, the most practical approach is to create a **Matrix** organization and for the project manager to borrow employees from the process managers and their departments. Make sure that the process managers provide a definite assignment to the employees with written instructions. Thus each process employee and the process manager will have a clear expectation regarding hours being devoted to the project and time away from the process workflow.

As project manager, you should prepare these instructions in coordination with the process managers. The process managers should be physically present at the initial project team-building and project launch meeting.

Performance disciplinary issues with employees in a matrix environment can be very complex. The process manager and the project manager will have to coordinate with the HR Department to determine who will take the lead in determining which manager will issue corrective actions if needed, approve time card adjustments, approve vacation time, or approve sick leave.

Summarizing Process Management and Project Management

As managerial skills grow, you will soon become recognized as a leader that has developed a highly competent and productive team of employees. Your reputation will spread. You can expect to be asked to accept higher levels of responsibility in processes and projects. Consequently, a Project Manager opportunity may appear. Currently, you probably are serving as a Process Manager. You must know the difference between process and project management before you can be effective as a Project Manager.

In the meeting where you are presented with the opportunity to accept a position as a Project Manager, you have to have a full understanding of the role to effectively negotiate the responsibilities, accountabilities, and authorities in serving in a dual role of being a process and project manager. As a Process Manager you have a firm grasp on the issues of managing a group of employees who complete repetitive tasks. Each management opportunity will provide you with the chance to make a significant contribution to the corporation.

Building a Career

USING A MENTOR

> *Definition of Mentor: A developmental partnership through which one person shares knowledge, skills, information and perspective to foster the growth of another. Considered a wise and trusted counselor, an influential senior sponsor or supporter.*

The primary function of a mentor is to assist you in your career development and in building career potential. You need to select a mentor from within the organization, another organization, a professional society, or a person you met at a conference or training class in whom you have cultivated a trusting friendship. There is a series of steps to be taken:

Make a personal decision that you have selected a career field that is compatible with your life goals.

- Evaluate the ethics, integrity, and honesty of business practices found in the current organization.
- Select a person who exhibits the same value system as you and occupies a position that you can aspire to achieve someday.

- Build trusting relationships with others; one based upon compatible life goals.
- Seek advice from the mentor when you are faced with important career-oriented decisions.
- Provide reciprocal opportunities and favors as deemed appropriate.
- Evaluate the career decisions the mentor has made and determine if comparable decisions are appropriate for your professional goals.

Getting a ticket punched in the organization

There are certain basic behaviors that will label you as a good manager, someone that is going places. We have provided a basic list of behaviors that will benefit you:

- Get to work early and leave work just after closing time. How early is early? Just be at your desk working 30 minutes before the scheduled time, we assume that you are not on a time clock, which brings its own set of behaviors.
- Leave work after the end of the workday. Some of you will be tempted to put in very long hours, expecting the supervisor or manager to notice you. Accomplish what is expected and agreed upon. Be careful – do not sacrifice personal time at home with friends or family.

> "Your work is going to fill a large part of your life, and the only way to be truly satisfied is to do what you believe is great work. And the only way to do great work is to love what you do. If you haven't found it yet, keep looking. Don't settle. As with all matters of the heart, you'll know when you find it."
>
> - Steve Jobs

- Control the workflow by accepting the assignments that can be accomplished.
- Maintain a dialogue with your supervisor regarding work progress.
- Accept a volunteer assignment such as an after-hours employee club or activity.
- Be prepared to present reports, never display shyness, or deference, look all straight in the eye, and answer with facts.

Finding career ladders and glass ceilings

In very large companies there are **career ladders** and **glass ceilings**. A career ladder provides an employee with a natural progression from a technical position to supervisor of a small group, to a manager of a single department, to a manager of a group of departments; onward and upward as your skills become noticed. However, with careful review of various managers and their "time-in-grade," you will soon recognize that some ladders have very few rungs and dead ends and some managers are stuck in their roles for perhaps years.

> "You are not here merely to make a living. You are here in order to enable the world to live more amply, with greater vision, with a finer spirit of hope and achievement. You are here to enrich the world, and you impoverish yourself if you forget the errand."
>
> - Woodrow Wilson

This phenomenon of limited opportunities is known as a glass ceiling; you can look upward and see through the ceiling, but may never be given access to the "next rung" or "floor above." To break through this ceiling requires different approaches. As discussed previously in this section, there are routes you can take, such as earning graduate degrees, receiving specialized certification, or using a mentor. Study carefully the attributers of those who have "broken through" the glass ceilings within the company. There is much to learn in observing the successful career paths of other managers.

Finding technical training – job performance enhancement

There will always be opportunities to learn new skills and acquire technical information that are useful on the job. The training falls into the following categories:

- **On the Job Training (OJT)** Those who have mastered a special procedure or process provide on-the-job training and are willing to spend time helping you.
- **Department Specific Training** The department you work in or the Human Resources Department provide special training that is specific to the job being performed.
- **In-House Seminars** One- or two-day seminars sponsored by and conducted in the organization's conference room or training facility. Upon completion, a certificate is awarded. Announcements of such seminars are provided in weekly news bulletins or special email notes. Watch carefully and have your name added to the routing lists.
- **Off-Site Seminars** One- or two-day seminars sponsored and conducted by an outside training company held in a conference room of a local hotel or convention center. Upon completion, a certificate is awarded.
- **Trade Conferences** Three- to five-day seminars sponsored and conducted by trade association held in a major resort conference center at a tourist destination such as Disneyworld, New York City, Boston, Washington DC, Hawaii, San Diego, or San Francisco. In some

cases, the conference may be in a location outside the boundaries of the United States such as Hong Kong, Tokyo, Rome, Paris, or London.

The last two described above are of special interest. They offer you opportunities for networking and establishing professional relationships with others in your career field. If such an opportunity should arise, make a point of accomplishing the following while attending a conference:

- Collect business cards. Enter the information into a personal electronic contact library or directory. Make a special note of the value of the contact to help you refresh your memory upon arrival back to work. Each contact you make could someday provide you with a critical piece of information needed to solve a complex problem or lead to other employment opportunities.
- Visit the products, services, and vendors displays in the exhibit hall. Bring a digital camera or camera phone and take pictures of products or services that will be useful to your company. E-mail the pictures plus descriptions of the items of interest back to the organization. Collect brochures and business cards. Again, each contact will be useful to you some day in the future; build a resource library of all materials collected. The companies with products on display may provide opportunities for a job change.

Measuring the value of education for the working adult

The world is now saturated with opportunities to earn a college degree using online learning.

The educational program advertisements promote: . . . *never attend class, work at your own pace, low cost, and submit homework using the internet. Earn your four year or graduate degree in one-half of the time and keep your full-time position. Apply the skills you learn in class directly to the work place. Student loans available!*

Such ads come to us on television, over the Internet, in magazines, and radio commercials. There are a few items you should consider when exploring the opportunity to earn a four-year college degree or graduate degree and selecting a college or university that offers educational training.

- **If everyone can earn the degree, then what is the value of the degree in the workplace?** The newspaper job ad will read: a four-year degree plus five years of experience. The purpose of the degree is to refine and expand personal problem-solving and analytical skills. The degree must emphasize speaking, communication, and writing abilities. The degree represents a significant milestone in life. A degree plus the experience separates you from those who have only the experience or just the degree.

- **Does the organization recognize a degree from the granting institution (school) that you are considering?** A check with the HR Department will give you information regarding which programs the company recognizes. If the degree is not considered credible by the organization, then attending the school is a significant waste of your money and time. Review very carefully the list from the HR Department of acceptable programs. Ask questions: Who assembled the list?' "What were the criteria the company used for deciding that a program is credible?

- **What is the history of the school, does it have a physical campus, are the faculty experts and experienced in their fields?** Academic incest can be a problem in educational degree programs. That is, colleges will hire their own graduates to fill teaching positions that in turn teach students who graduate and are then hired to teach in the same programs. And the story continues. Review the literature the school publishes and request a copy of the faculty roster and the listing of their earned degrees. If members of the faculty have earned their degrees from the same school that they are teaching at then be careful.

- **What percentage of managers have degrees and what schools did they attend?** Some organizations have highly entrenched educational cultures others do not. Ask around the work area and do a quick survey: who has college degrees, what are their degree fields, what schools granted their degrees. The managers above you – did they earn their promotions with or without their degrees? What role did the college degree play in their achieving the higher paid position? If the organization places a low value on an earned degree and your degree is from a nationally recognized public or private university, then you may want to consider finding employment with an organization that more closely aligns with your personal life's goals and expectations.

NETWORKING AND CAREER GROWTH

An important opportunity for career growth is networking. Through informal relationships you will be informed of opportunities; take the time to evaluate each opportunity and be sure to return the favor. Professional organizations serve as a common meeting place for networking.

Using professional associations and memberships
– purpose and opportunities

Professional associations exist to bring people together who have common interests. The *Encyclopedia of Associations* is a directory of professional associations, available on the internet that you can use to identify an association that supports your professional interests or career. A brief listing of professional associations is provided in the appendix of this book. Use the Internet and Google to search for the web page for an organization of interest. The web page provides a mission statement, charter, and contact information for the association.

Professional associations generally have local chapters with monthly meetings and guest speakers of interest. Each local chapter supports the state and national association. The chapter sponsors conferences, special training, and "meet-and-greet" events. Within the local chapter, officers are elected and volunteer projects are carried out during the year. The leadership of a chapter is usually structured with volunteers for the leadership positions of president, vice president, treasurer, program chair, and new membership chair. The officers and board are voted in by the chapter membership and usually serve for one- to three-year terms. An annual membership fee is required. With the membership comes a subscription to the national journal and reduced fees for attending the annual conventions or conferences.

> "You have to be burning with 'an idea, or a problem, or a wrong that you want to right.' If you're not passionate enough from the start, you'll never stick it out."
>
> - Steve Jobs

Networking within a professional association

With the membership comes the invitation to attend the local weekly or monthly meetings. The meetings have a regular list of activities. An evening program is usually held at a local hotel conference room or restaurant dining room. You can expect

the following agenda. Knowing how the evening progresses will help you feel at ease. The typical agenda may appear as follows:
- Arrival and "attitude adjustment" (unwind from the stresses of the business day) for a time to meet and greet.
- Meeting is called to order and chapter announcements made by the president. Upcoming special events are discussed, new members introduced, and guest speakers presented.
- Before-dinner speaker – a short presentation covering the theme for the evening.
- Dinner – meal served and table conversations continue.
- After dinner keynote speaker – explores the evening's theme in greater detail.
- Evening closure – time to continue casual conversations and leave.

A chapter that has a noontime meeting will not have two speakers and the lunch hour governs the length of time for the meeting.

The meeting provides you with the opportunity to meet fellow professionals. The guest speakers give insights regarding changes in the law, technology, or consumer patterns. You are provided with numerous possibilities to build professional relationships, to meet key leaders in the field, and to discuss work related issues over lunch or dinner, Chapters typically have career-networking newsletters. This gives you insights regarding possible career opportunities.

Listing of a few professional associations

The list in the appendix was derived from an Internet search.

Additional professional associations can be found through searching the *Encyclopedia of Associations*.

DISCOVERING THAT A CAREER LADDER IS LEANING AGAINST THE WRONG BUILDING

- There will be a point in time that brings a realization your career and profession is in need of change. Perhaps a series of ethical decisions made by the organization, a downturn in the economy brings a reduction to the labor force, a competitor creates new products to the market place, or there are no longer career challenges for you. Any one of these may give you a clear message that is time to reposition your career ladder.

Producing the plan

So, you have concluded that your ladder to success is leaning against the wrong building and it is time to change employers and move on. Regardless of the reasons, you decide that it is time to start "the search." Most valuable to you will be the network of professional friends or work associates who can provide confidential information and leads for job opportunities. Remember all of the business cards you have been collecting? Now is the time to review them. Once you generate two or three very strong possibilities – ones that you can seriously consider – then the following steps are recommended. Additionally, social network sites are available and provide opportunities to reach out to contacts.

> "It's better to hang out with people better than you. Pick out associates whose behavior is better than yours and you'll drift in that direction."
>
> - Warren Buffett

There are a couple of secrets hidden in the steps below to creating a successful job interview and receiving an offer of employment. The suggestions are based upon the authors' combined 50+ years of experience of having interviewed and hired more than 300 people. Rarely did we find that an applicant came to the interview properly prepared. From this perspective we offer the approach discussed below for interview preparation process:

Getting organized – a preparatory step

As a new applicant you will need to purchase a 3-ring binder with page separators for a filing system, which you will use and will take with you to the interview. The ring binder is divided into three sections using the page separators:

Section 1 of the ring binder – Your resume and a copy of the job description

Section 2 of the ring binder – Company related research – economic performance

Section 3 of the ring binder – Company related research – news or press releases

Preparing a custom-designed resume

Review the job description very carefully and make a list of every requirement. Do not leave any requirement untouched. Type each requirement into a Microsoft Word© document. This page becomes the first page of your resume. Under each job description requirement, list your previous or current professional experience and successes. This demonstrates that you have the skill and ability to fulfill each responsibility listed in the job description on the first day of employment. Use one font style for the job description requirements. Then change to another to list your experiences. This approach provides for very easy reading for the person reviewing your resume.

Next, within the text that describes your professional experience, it is critical that you describe how the efforts resulted in that activity running smoother, faster, better, nicer, easier, greater, and with higher quality. Here explain in short sentences how the work environment, *because of your presence,* was improved with greater quality and productivity. This discussion of the successes you achieved is most important. The writing is very difficult work but stick with the task!

With this custom-designed resume, you want to show that you are a perfect fit for this new position. That you will provide the same intensity and urgency for every responsibility that is entrusted to you. You want to show a one-to-one correlation between the job description and your skill set. You have removed all doubt regarding the possible fit – you and the new job opportunity.

You have proven that, when hired, the department, section, division, or small work group will run smoother, better, grander, and with an increased level of productivity. You have provided all of the analysis and matching of your professional skills to the job description. So many job applicants leave this analysis of matching a generic resume to the job description up to the interviewer. Again, on this first page you have proven you are the perfect match for the position.

The second page of the resume contains the standard brief historical work history, education, special training, and other pieces of relevant information.

This first section of the ring binder also contains copies of other supporting documentation such as:

- DMV driving record (if requested in job description).
- Education transcripts for posted college degrees.
- Certificates of completion for technical or managerial training.
- US or Foreign Passports copies.
- DD-214 (If military experience exists).
- State certificates, licenses or permits.
- Documentation of proficiencies in foreign language(s).
- Certificates of membership in professional societies relating to business or of professional interest.
- Certificates for volunteer time in the community such as Girl Scouts, Boy Scouts, 4H, FFA, PTA, tutoring at the local public or private school, community policing, hospital patient care, homeless shelter, Meals-On-Wheels, etc.
- Certificates of efforts made to local not-for-profit agencies.

Completing the corporate financial research

It is now time to prepare the material that will go into the second section of the ring binder. Do a Google search of the company name. Find the corporate website and identify the company history, its primary products/and or services provided, number of divisions. Knowing the company's SIC number will be helpful in the search for information.

If it is **publicly traded company** on one of the stock exchanges, then with a little effort investigating the Security Exchange Commission's financial databases, you will be able to get the ticker symbol and a copy of the company's current Quarterly Financial Report. This will provide the Corporate Income and Balance Sheet, letter from the President/CEO or CFO summarizing the current state of financial health of the company, and the trend line for the traded stock's performance.

Also, the members of the Corporate Board of Directors will be listed. With the data you will be able to discuss the strengths and weaknesses of the company during the interview.

If it is a **privately held company,** then public quarterly financial reports will not be available. However, with an online search you will be able to determine if the company is listed in trade journals, magazines, or financial newspapers. Much can be learned from business reviews or editorials. Make notes of important facts relating to the company's standing among its competitors.

With a little reading, you will be able to determine the state of economic health for the company, the current business environment, and its prospects for future growth and ability to deal with the competition.

Completing the corporate publicity research

This last step involves the discovery of local news press releases that provide insights regarding the company's "civic mindedness." What has the company returned to the community? Does the company regularly sponsor not-for-profit organizations? Does it organize walks for cancer research, kids' soccer teams, bicycle classics, high school career day, and internships for college students? Assemble as much information as possible. This will be used in the "small talk" phase, a critical part of the interview.

> "I saw the angel in the marble and carved until I set him free."
>
> - Michelangelo

Getting through a successful interview

The date for the interview has arrived. The following discussion is designed to help you anticipate the interview and execute each step successfully. The interview is usually divided into four phases. It is very important that you recognize each interview phase and move smoothly from one phase to another. The data you collected, organized, and placed in the ring binder is now ready for use during the interview.

Interview – Getting to know you and small talk

You may have to face an interview committee. A committee all asking you questions can be difficult. Take one question at a time and show sincerity in each answer. The interviewer and each member of the committee will want to get to know you and appraise the level of comfort with the process and your general presence. Do you appear to be quiet, timid, shy, overly aggressive, loud, or commanding? There is the unspoken question: "How will you fit into the existing organization's culture and social structure?" Your research in the third section of your ring binder now comes to play. During this "get to know you" small talk period, you have the opportunity to discuss the company's history, significant accomplishments, and position in the market place.

The manager(s) conducting the interview are very proud of the organization. During this introductory phase, you can share in this pride and establish a commonality between you and the interviewer. This step quickly establishes you as a credible candidate who acknowledges the value of the company's contribution to the community. This could be the time you are considered to be a worthy candidate based upon the "small talk." Do not act surprised if the interview shifts to your favor at this point.

Interview – Match to the job description

You need to recognize this transition, if you do not, awkwardness will be created which will lead to discrediting you even with the advances made during the first phase. You have already analyzed every aspect of the job description and established perfect fit to the job requirements. This phase will be dedicated to you showing the interviewer how much you contributed to the last organization and you will do the same for the new position. The critical point is to establish the negotiation position that you are capable of performing all tasks in the job description. At the same time you have the skills to implement programs to improve productivity and quality. The analysis of the job description will display you as a serious candidate who will be productive on the first day.

> "Being powerful is like being a lady. If you have to tell people you are, you aren't!"
>
> - Margaret Thatcher

Interview – Match to the company structure

You now are ready to show how much you know about the company. You should know the total number of employees, products and or services produced, how the organization is divided into sections or divisions, and who are the leading competitors. In most generic interviews, the interviewer will spend a lot of time describing to the candidate all of the aspects of the organization. Since you have already established an in-depth knowledge, there is an opportunity for you to refocus the interview back to you being the best candidate. By knowing the structure of the organization you can demonstrate a comfort in being a part of their large, complex organization and how you can be productive on the first day. Dropping a few names of key individuals in the organization will help as well.

Interview – Graceful exit

You can expect the interviewer to say, "Do you have any questions?" The interviewer is giving you a signal that the interview is ending. We suggest that you only pose one question for clarification. Then take a minute to summarize why you are the best candidate. Ask directly when you can expect to receive information regarding their final decision regarding the selection. If you feel it is appropriate, leave the ring binder with the interviewer.

Considering the key points in the interview

The ring binder, the custom resume, the corporate research, and application of experience demonstrate the quality of work that the interviewer can expect you to generate for the company. You have established yourself as the ideal candidate. One who will produce high quality effort. You are prepared to make the work environment better and will create a team of employees capable of being proactive and productive.

You have demonstrated a willingness to go **"above and beyond"** for the company. With the economic conditions in business **"going above and beyond"** is considered the rule of the day. This attitude and culture means the difference between survival and failure of an entire organization. Your resume has demonstrated your support of the **"above and beyond"** attitude.

In this interview remember.

"You only have one chance to make a first impression."

Stocking the Manager's Tool Box

Applying strategic change

A manager must be an agent of change. The department and employees must demonstrate improvement, refinement of processes, and increase productivity. Opportunities bring the necessity for change. You, as the manager, will be faced with the daunting task of instituting change within the work group. The following illustrates a series of steps for accomplishing change:

The key to remember is that for change to occur, you as the manager must work to destabilize the existing environment. For some, perhaps the analogy is to "unfreeze" the current process or procedure, make the change, and then "refreeze" with the new process in place

According to The Change Formula as was created by Richard Beckhard and David Gleicher and is called Gleicher's Formula there are two sides of the strategic change equation. On the left side is your effort to raise the **employees' dissatisfaction with the status quo,** provide a **practical**

first step, and communicate a **vision for the future** that the change will bring. On the right side of the equation are the employees' expressions of **resistance to change**. This resistance is a combination of **fear** of the required additional effort to be expended, **the cost**, and not willing accept the vision for the future.

Facing the most difficult task – accomplishing change

You will be faced with the need to implement change to improve productivity, efficiency, quality, or assume new or expanded responsibilities. You have to elevate the employees' **Dissatisfaction with the Status Quo** and you must take the **Practical First Step**. This will require careful thought and planning. By producing the first step, the employees realize the change they face is the result of your diligent planning and commitment to success. Of equal importance is for you to present the **Desired End State** or vision of the future – what the future will look like once the change is in place.

> "The greatest leader is not necessarily the one who does the greatest things. He is the one that gets the people to do the greatest things."
>
> - Ronald Reagan

However, a proposed change always brings **Resistance** from the employees. The resistance can be easily heard from the employees. The new change will require too much **Time**, too much **Effort**, and the expressed **Fear** of the unknown. Successful change requires the assembling of a strategy that creates an off-balance condition for the environment.

Implementation of a successful change may take days, weeks, or even months. You, as the strategic change agent, have to be diligent, unattached emotionally to the process, and be prepared for a long and often very tedious journey.

Suggestion: use the approach above to examine the history of previous successful and unsuccessful changes that have taken place in your organization. Take a failed change process and carefully dissect each element and determine why the change failed. Look at the role of the manager, how the change (vision) was communicated, how it was presented, and how it was worked, and the power of the employees who successfully resisted the change. You now have the opportunity to learn from the past errors or misjudgments, and you are ready to build a change strategy wired for success![12,13]

Managing and being a change agent

During the first few months, you will have identified areas that are in need of change. The fine-tuning of the organization is an important responsibility for you the manager. The tasks of changing employees' attitudes, employee performance, procedures, policies, room layout, use of tools, work schedules, filing systems, and reporting of accountabilities will be of benefit to the group.

The most notable impact of a successful change will be on the employees and their performances. The employees soon realize that a light is now shining brightly on the "old ways" of acceptable low performance and poor quality. Employees with good performance will take pride in their new set of accomplishments brought on by the strategic change. They know that the organization and you, their manager, are refusing to "look the other way." The Critical Success Factors when blended with the strategic change plan provides a foundation for guiding your group to higher levels of performance.

Applying Lean Six Sigma and Continuous Quality Improvement

Defining Lean Six Sigma

Six Sigma is an approach to improving the performance of a work group, department, division, or organization.

Learning about Lean

Lean is the application of a set of principles whose objective is to eliminate waste while improving the process flow in order to achieve speed and agility at lower cost. It is based upon the premise that all work contains some amount of waste or non-value added effort. A Lean program defines and seeks to remove seven forms of waste.

Seven areas of waste:
- **Correction** – correcting or repairing defects in parts or materials. The paid overtime to employees to rework defective product.
- **Overproduction** – producing more pieces or services than are needed. Consumption of additional raw materials and labor to produce product that requires additional storage space. Results in overuse of machines and employees.
- **Process** – processing work that has no connection to advancing the production or improving quality. Additional steps in the manufacturing of product that do not add value to the finished item.
- **Conveyance** – moving of product that does not add or contribute to its value. Important to avoid the movement of product that does not satisfy the just-in-time delivery.
- **Inventory** – generating unnecessary or unneeded product that takes up space and requires additional

energy to move it. Defective product may remain hidden within the finished goods holdings.
- **Motion** – moving people or machinery that does not contribute to added value. The distance between operations that creates excessive walking for employees or transport of goods.
- **Waiting** – creating idle time for employees and or product between operations or events. An idle machine waiting for an employee to load new parts. An idle employee waiting to begin the next step in a process.

Defining Six Sigma

Six Sigma is the application of principles whose objective is to eliminate **defects** and **variation** within a process.

Six Sigma training is divided into the study of the levels of proficiency and problem-solving. Training is accomplished and examinations are taken to demonstrate skills mastered. There are certain roles played in the Six Sigma process. The roles are listed below

> **Six Sigma – Executive Team:** Owns the business, produces the vision, and sets expectations for the organization
>
> **Six Sigma – Deployment Leader:** Manages the Six Sigma program and sets the implementation of a Six Sigma program into motion
>
> **Six Sigma – Champion:** Recognizes problem areas of the business, defines projects, and assigns projects. Responsible for the business roadmap and employee training plan

> "Whenever there is fear, you will get wrong figures."
>
> - W. Edwards Deming

Six Sigma – Master Black Belt: Considered the technical expert using the Six Sigma methodology. Mentors Black Belts and supports the Champions

Six Sigma – Black Belt Serves as a project team leader, working on problems that have a high financial return to the company when solved

Six Sigma – Green Belt Solves less complex problems within their span of control and can serve on a Black Belt's team helping to complete a Black Belt's project

Six Sigma – Yellow Belt Entry level in training and skill level, Able to identify simple problems, collect data and do analysis with the help of others.

Six Sigma Project Phases

A Six Sigma problem-solving project lead by a Black Belt and supported by a Green Belt and Yellow Belt is divided into the following five phases often referred to as the DMAIC:

[D] DEFINE Phase: The problem is identified and the surrounding environment is described

[M] MEASURE Phase: A data collection process is created, data collected to identify an operational benchmark.

[A] ANALYSIS Phase: The data are charted or graphed to identify the degree of variability and the degree to which the product quality fails to meet the acceptable standard

[I] IMPROVE Phase: A program is created to change the existing condition and establish an output that meets the standard

[C] CONTROL Phase: A program is created to make

sure the improvement phase continues and quality standards are not permitted to deteriorate.

Summarizing Lean Six Sigma

Lean removes the **seven forms of waste** so that **Six Sigma** can focus on eliminating **defects** and **variation** in the process. Six Sigma is a method to create or change processes to make them more capable. Thus, the relationship exists between the two methodologies Lean and Six Sigma for improving organizational performance. Take the time to find texts that define the quality processes of Lean and Six Sigma. Time invested in earning the Six Sigma Black Belt certification and earning the title will pay dividends that will span your entire career.

OBSERVING AN ORGANIZATION'S CULTURE

Listing of the symbols of organizational culture

The organizational culture is composed of complex and interlocking concepts and behaviors, which are listed below.[14] In time, you will begin to identify the symbols of your organization's culture. You can use organizational culture symbols during conversations with employees, in staff meetings, and in presentations. The symbols give you a tool to communicate with employees, convey special information, and to appreciate the meaning the organization has to its employees. Each symbol listed below has value and importance.

Myths

Myths are narratives that anchor the present to the past. They usually originate in the founding or launching of an enterprise and the myths transform a place of work into a revered institution for the employees.

Values

Values define what an organization stands for, those qualities worthy of esteem or commitment. They create a sense of identity from the boardroom to the factory floor, sometimes even capturing the company mission statement.

Vision

Vision turns an organization's core ideology or sense of purpose into an image of what the future might become. It is a shared fantasy that illuminates new possibilities within the realm of the existing values.

Stories and Fairy Tales

Stories and fairy tales offer comfort, reassurance, direction, and hope to all employees. Sometimes providing more entertainment rather than truth or wisdom, and they convey information, morals, values, and myths vividly and convincingly and are commonly told and retold during social events or group meetings.

Story telling is a simple, memorable, and timeless way of doing the following:
- Pass along corporate traditions
- Train employees
- Empower people
- Recognize accomplishments
- Spread the word
- Have fun
- Recruit and hire the right people
- Develop managers and employees

Rituals

Rituals are the simple day-to-day routines that become the "dance of life." They help people face and confront the unpredictability of present and future events. Rituals create order and clarity and play important roles in binding the members of a group together.

Ceremony

Ceremonies are grander, more elaborate, and less frequent occasions than rituals that consist of special moments in life that conveys special meanings. They have four roles: socialize, stabilize, reassure, and convey messages to external constituencies. Within ceremony special forms of dress, seating arrangements, and the display of symbols such as logos, awards, or pictures are present.

Metaphor, Humor and Play

As an overview, these three are the indirect ways for people to grapple with issues that are too complex, mysterious, or threatening to confront head on.

Metaphor

Metaphor compresses complicated issues into understandable images, influencing attitudes, evaluations, and actions. For example, managers who see themselves as physicians are likely to differ in their approaches towards their employees from managers who see their work as timekeepers and disciplinarians.

Humor

Humor plays a number of important functions. It integrates, expresses skepticism, and contributes to flexibility. Humor can socialize, convey membership, establish solidarity, or facilitate face-saving.

Play

Play permits the relaxing of roles to explore alternatives and encourages experimentation, and flexibility. Five guidelines for use of play to accomplish work in an organization are as follows:
- Treat goals as hypotheses – Goals should be considered only as possibilities and opportunities.
- Treat intuition as real – Initiative feelings represent personal feelings and cannot be ignored.
- Treat hypocrisy as transition – Hypocrisy will in time pass and may only be vaguely remembered.
- Treat memory as an enemy – Memory changes over time and cannot be trusted.
- Treat experiences as a theory – Personal experiences may prove to be false and may not be relied on.

With time and your improved observation skills all items listed above will be observed within your organization. You will have a new vocabulary that will describe the simple actions and conversations of members of organization.

Studying the elements of organization culture

Careful review of the employees' attitudes, behaviors, and productivity will provide you with those elements that you may want to change or delete from the daily routines of the department. There will be elements within the department that you perceive to be counterproductive. With the list above you will have a set of cultural lenses to evaluate the work day. As a manager this may appear to be a microscopic analysis of the department. The goal is to improve the productivity of the department and evaluate each aspect of the department's culture that could be detrimental to the performance of the group. The department's established rituals and ceremonies may be counter to your approach in managing the group. Walk with care down this path. The resistance to change may produce a set of very complex problems.

LOOKING AT SUCCESSFUL ORGANIZATIONS

Measuring the seven practices of successful organizations

There are indicators that can be used to define and measure successful organizations, below are attributes worthy of consideration.[15] Successful organizations will display the following seven characteristics. Evaluate each item below as it exists in the organization and within your department:

1. **Employment security**
Produce very careful hiring strategies, people are not considered to be expendable tools.

2. **Selective hiring**
Expend funds to create a good applicant pool; care is exercised in placement of new hires.

Search for primary attributes such as ethics, character, attitude, honesty, work ethic.

Monitor effectiveness of placement process and hold hiring manager responsible for new employee performance.

3. **Self-managed teams**
Control work and pool ideas and the whole are greater than the sum of the parts.

Remove layers of management.

4. **Compensation related to performance**
Display the relationship between pay and performance is recognized by the employees.

5. **Training**
Invest in training to improve work performance of employees.

6. **Reduction in status or position titles**
Change in position titles was a manager is now a coach.

7. **Sharing information**
Trust employees with organizational information.

Evaluating a group's effectiveness and maturity

As a manager, you need a tool to measure and evaluate your own effectiveness and that of the workgroup. You probably realize that the employees will eventually mirror your behaviors, work ethic, and standards. The characteristics of effectiveness provided below are really a measurement of you as their leader. When considering each item, be very honest and critique with care.[16,17]

Group effectiveness

Participation	[Few dominate or excluded]	or	[All are listened to]
Feelings	[Hidden, ignored, criticized]	or	[Freely expressed]
Trust	[Fear, distrust, guarded actions]	or	[Freedom to express trust]

Creativity and Growth	[Rigid roles stereotyped]	or	[Flexible & improvement]
Leadership	[Depend on one person]	or	[Distribute leadership]
Decisions	[Avoided]	or	[Timely & supported]
Goals	[Confused, diverse, conflicting]	or	[Clear to all]

Group maturity

Another level of analysis you as a manager need to use is to measure the level of maturity that exists within your work group. Also evaluate the environments created by fellow managers in neighboring departments. The check list below will provide interesting insights regarding the makeup of the employees. This list will provide you with opportunities to begin the process of analysis of your group's maturity level. A mature group will in turn produce high levels of employee satisfaction and productivity. The following characteristics should be observed:

- Clear communication channels
- Adequate mechanisms for getting feedback
- Acceptance of minority views
- Adequate decision making procedures
- Shared participation in leadership functions
- Optimal group cohesion
- Maximum use of member resources
- Feelings of interdependence with authority persons
- Clear goals accepted by each members
- Flexible organizational policies and procedures

New employee's perceptions

One often overlooked area is the study of the perceptions held by new hires within your work group. The following questions will be asked quietly by the new hire upon entering the work group and evaluating this new environment.

- Identity – Who am I to be in this work group?
- Control and Influence – Can I influence others in the work group or will I be ignored?
- Needs and Goals – Are the group goals and my goals compatible?
- Acceptance and intimacy – Will I as the new employee be liked in this group?

The above questions create a critique of your managerial style and the work environment you create for accepting new hires. An honest self-appraisal of your impact on new hires which may be painful has to be accomplished. Identify areas that need improvement and go to work making the repairs. Return frequently to this list of questions to monitor the progress being made to improve the work environment for new hires. Frequent turnover in new hires produces additional overhead costs.

INTERVIEWING APPLICANTS FOR MANAGEMENT POSITIONS

In time you will be asked to join an interview panel to select a new manager. Being a member of a committee to interview and hire a new manager can be a daunting task. The following interview questions are provided to give a different perspective on evaluating candidates for a management position.[18]

- A manager's daily work is similar to that of a piano tuner. A piano tuner begins by listening and determining which strings are out of tune. Then through a process of tightening, loosening, replacing broken or stretched strings, the piano slowly becomes tuned. The tuning process requires that there be an accepted tone for each string. When struck, this set of standards becomes the criteria for performance for all piano strings. Once in tune, the piano can produce music. As a manager-piano tuner, which areas of our organization have you observed as being out of tune? By what standard would you make that decision to determine the degree of tuning required?

- Within the organization, you will identify areas that are out of tune, and then make decisions regarding functions that need tuning (improving). What is the systematic process for implementing a strategic change within a group of employees so that a harmonious work environment is maintained while important changes (tuning) are being implemented?
- One symptom of an entire organization that is out of tune is dissatisfied employees. What symptoms do you look for as indicators that employee dissatisfaction with work environment is steadily increasing? How do you measure the degree of employees' satisfaction or dissatisfaction?
- A piano tuner will have to replace broken strings. The piano tuner seeks to replace the strings with those of the highest possible quality. When seeking new employees to fill an open position, what do you consider to be the three most important characteristics you will look for in a manager?
- Describe, from past experiences, the most complex tuning process that you accomplished within an organization. What brought about the need for change and what was the eventual outcome of the change? Looking back on the experience what could you have done differently and would the outcome be the same?

- Describe personal goals and activities that will lead to improving your skills as a manager.
- From your perspective what is the difference between being an administrator, a manager, a supervisor, a leader, or a director? Can you give examples of each to illustrate the differences?

Measuring personal value systems

A quick and simple approach to determine the employees' value systems is to measure them. The measuring process identifies potential areas of conflict between employees' values. First, ask the employees to rank the items on the list below, and then you compare your personal ranking to theirs. Once completed, a comparison will demonstrate the similarities and differences in the values that exist within the work group.

Your knowledge of their value system will enable you to design a strategy that will protect you from serious leadership errors and conflict. For example, if you spend time building an elaborate employee recognition program [**your value system**] when all the employees' want is a flexible time off policy [**their value system**], there is a probability that a serious conflict might occur.

As another example, you may expend much effort designing and implementing public displays of rank, when what the employees actually want is a competitive salary and modern tools. Much of the turmoil within a work environment can be traced back to the conflict between rankings of values and the importance of the

> "The way to get things done is not to mind who gets the credit for doing them."
>
> - Benjamin Jowett

values held by each employee in the work group as compared to yours.

Use the list below to create a survey to administer to the employees.[19] But, proceed with care and caution. Check with HR and your supervisor to determine if a survey is appropriate within your organization. There may be strict policies that prohibit the distribution of surveys to employees. If a survey is possible select a small group to measure value systems.

The list below contains common values held by employees related to the work place. You can edit, expand, or alter the list to fit the work place employees. The values represent the diversity of the dynamics of personal feelings. For some, a competitive salary far outweighs the need to publicly display of rank or position.

Rank order the following in level of importance[19]

1 = Most important
10 = Least important

_____ A.   Competitive salary
_____ B.   Open and honest promotional opportunities
_____ C.   Public recognition for excellent performance
_____ D.   Public display of rank
_____ E.   Competitive benefits
_____ F.   Safe work environment
_____ G.   Modern tools
_____ H.   Honest and sincere performance appraisals
_____ I.   Flexible time off policies
_____ J.   Encouragement to experiment

Once the items are ranked an employee's value system can be identified. Much effort can be expended by a manager implementing work area improvements but which are discovered to be rejected by employees.

To illustrate value systems, as an example, the author has taught applied business statistics in a graduate degree program in business. Homework papers are graded each week and returned to the students. For one week the papers were divided into two groups. Those papers that were neatly prepared with correct answers and the second group those of lesser quality. A small gold star was placed on each paper within the first group.

At the beginning of class the papers were returned to the students and little thought given to the gold stars or who received them. Within a few minutes one of the students became very emotional and left the room. Upon talking to the student, she explained that she waited from kindergarten to her senior year of high school to get just one gold star on her homework but it never came. Now years later she received a gold star on her statistics homework. The value she placed on receiving the gold star far out ranked other reward systems in the class. Do not under estimate the value of giving a "gold star." Simple gestures are important to employees!

Conclusion

THIS HANDBOOK, AS STATED in the beginning, has been designed to give you a simple and practical set of tools to practice the art and science of managing others. For some, the craft of managing may appear to be a gift and tasks are carried out with success. For other managers it is a constant struggle and good things sometimes happen. And, others seem never to get it right and their work groups remain in a constant state of disarray.

Being a successful manager takes practice, patience, persistence, and a perception of a desired future. You must be able to emotionally step outside of difficult situations, detach yourself from the feelings of others, and evaluate and create a plan to improve the situation.

A secret of being a successful manager is the ability to assume the role of being a "servant-leader." As a leader, you are also a servant to the work group. You create the clean, safe, stable, predictable, and practical work environment for your employees. You provide the tools, equipment, work surfaces, compensation, and training. Your hard work, often invisible to the employees, produces the environment that you and the employees will be proud to own. Abraham Lincoln once stated,

"I like to see a man proud of the place in which he lives. I like to see a man live so that his place will be proud of him."

You have much to anticipate. Being a successful manager provides you with rewards the employees will never see or experience. It is worth the time and effort, Persevere. In time you will master the art of managing others and confidently return the answer *"Yes, I am your new manager!"*

Appendix

CLASSIC WRITINGS

As a manager you will need to develop a small library of classics for reading.

There are a few writings which seem to capture the essence of leadership principles. The books describe with remarkable accuracy very useful leadership techniques. There is no attempt here to explain the theories, but to briefly describe them in the hopes that you may find them of use. Each of the two texts mentioned here deserve thoughtful reading. The work by Sun Tzu is a must read!

The Art of War – Sun Tzu, 400 B.C.[20]
"When the troops are in disarray only the general is to blame"

WE PROVIDE THIS LITTLE excerpt from the text because it discusses an important description of human behavior. It is sad to think that we have not changed in 2,000 years, but it is a comfort also.

Sun Tzu's *Art of War*, written in China more than 2,000 years ago, is the first known attempt to formulate a rational basis for the planning and conduct of military operations. The essays have never been surpassed in comprehensiveness and depth of understanding. His writings consists of the concentrated essence of wisdom on the conduct of war. The text contains principles still acted upon by modern military leaders.

Sun Tzu's writings are a recognized application for managing an organization. The work's popularity as a classic piece of literature is ever increasing. Below are quotes, taken from *The Art of War* and then edited by the authors of this text and applied to the supervisor-employee relationship.

Terrain, Chapter 10: 18

[18] When the general is weak and without authority; when his orders are not clear and distinct; when there are no fixed duties assigned to officers and men, and the ranks are formed in a slovenly manner, the result is utter disorganization.

[18] When the manager is weak and without authority; when the orders are not clear and distinct; when there are no fixed duties assigned to supervisors and employees, and the work areas are maintained in a slovenly manner, the result is utter disorganization.

Estimates, Chapter 1: 9

[9] The Commander stands for the virtues of sincerity, benevolence, courage, and strictness.

[9] The manager stands for the virtues of sincerity, benevolence, courage, and strictness.

Marches, Chapter 9: 42, 43, 44, 45

[42] If soldiers are punished before they have grown attached to you,

they will not prove submissive; they will be practically useless. If, when the soldiers have become attached to you, punishments are not enforced, they will still be useless.

[42] If employees are disciplined before they have grown attached to you, they will not prove submissive; they will be practically useless. If, when the employees have become attached to you, reprimands are not enforced, they will still be useless.

[43] Therefore soldiers must be treated in the first instance with humanity, but kept under control by means of iron discipline. This is a certain road to victory.

[43] Therefore employees must be treated in the first instance with humanity, but kept under control by means of carefully crafted policies and procedures. This is a certain means to achieve success.

[44] If in training, soldiers' commands are habitually enforced, the army will be well disciplined; if not, its discipline will be bad.

[44] If in training, instructions to employees are habitually enforced, the work group will be well disciplined; if not, its discipline will be bad. Instructions must be followed.

[45] If a general shows confidence in his men but always insists on his orders being obeyed, the gain will be mutual.

[45] If a manager shows confidence in his employees but always insists on instructions being obeyed, the gain will be mutual.

Estimates, Chapter 1: 26

[26] Now, the general who wins a battle makes many calculations in his temple ere the battle is fought.

[26] Now, the manager who wins an advantage makes

calculations, builds models, and develops strategies before the competition's market position is challenged.

The Prince by Machiavelli

Another good book to read is *The Prince* by Machiavelli. We caution you to read the book itself; do not read someone else's interpretation or commentaries until you have read the full work. We limit our comments to this one: Machiavelli had both a hard and soft approach to managing, he did not recommend either, but did recommend that you understand the consequences of your actions.

Resource Materials

The following publications are worthy of consideration for regular reading. As a manager, you must read regularly business publications in order to continually develop your base of knowledge, leadership skills, and technical expertise in managing the work of others. From an intense reading program, current trends in the fields of research and development, marketing and sales, finance and accounting, manufacturing, and product distribution systems can be identified and applied to your. Review the listing of resource materials. With personal research you will want to insert additional publications to the list.

Appendix A – Business and management journals

The authors suggest that a new manager subscribe to a business or management journal and read regularly. A partial listing of important journals in the field is provided below. Select one or two journals of interest, subscribe, and ready regularly. Identify journal's that pertain to your industry.

ABA Journal

Accounting & Marketing

Advances in International Management

Asia-Pacific Journal of Management

Business & Legal Sciences

Corporate Governance: An International Review

Cross-Cultural Research

Emergence: Complexity & Organization

Entrepreneurship & Organizational Management

European Journal of International Management

Global Strategy Journal

Harvard Business Review

Hotel & Business Management

Human Organization

International Business Review

International Journal of Management and Business Studies

Journal of International Business Studies

Journal of International Economics

Journal of International Management

Journal of World Business

Management International Review

Multinational Business Review

Organizational Development Journal

Performance Improvement

Public Administration Quarterly

Quality Progress

Strategic Finance

Tourism & Hospitality

Training Journal

Appendix B – Business magazines and newspapers

A subscription to a daily or weekly business magazine and or newspaper is an important part of career development and becoming knowledgeable in specific field of business. Being aware of the current trends and changes in the business climate is critical for a new manager. Partial list of publications are listed below.

Ad Week (Industry & Trade Magazine

Advertising Age (Industry & Trade Magazine)

Barron's

Business Section – Los Angeles Times

Business Section – New York Times

Business Section – USA Today

Business Section – Washington Post

Business Wire

BusinessWeek

Economics & Business Week

Economics Week

Entrepreneur

Fast Company

Financial Times

Forbes

Fortune

Health Risk Factor Week

Healthcare Finance, Tax & Law Weekly

Healthcare Mergers, Acquisitions & Ventures Week

Home Business Magazine

Hong Kong Economic Times

HR Focus

Inc.

Investor Business Daily

Journal of Commerce

Kiplinger's Personal Finance

Law & Health Weekly

Leadership Excellence

Leisure & Travel Business

Money

The Economist

Wall Street Journal

Appendix C – Business and management books

A well-read manager will maintain a professional library of current and classic. Time invested in a regular reading program will pay future dividends. The Dilbert books and Who Moved My Cheese are listed to provide the lighter side of managing others. Over time you will gravitate toward a select set of authors and titles that peak your interest. The *New York Times Best Seller List* should be reviewed. Perhaps develop a book sharing program with fellow managers. The key: do not stop looking for the next "great book."

7 Habits of Successful People by Stephen R. Covey

A Behavioral Theory of the Firm by R.M. Cyert and A.G. March

Attitude is Everything by Paul J. Meyer

Blue Ocean Strategy by W. Chen Kim and Renee Maubiogne

Dilbert's Guide to the Rest of Your Life Dispatches from Cubicleland by Scott Adams

Good to Great – Why Some Companies Make the Leap and Others Do Not by Jim Collins

Magnetic Leadership – Are you a good enough leader to be hired by your best employees? by Vic Downing, Global Advantage, Inc.

How the Mighty Fall and Why Some Companies Never Give In by Jim Collins

Primal Leadership Learning to Lead with Emotional Intelligence by Daniel Goleman, Richard Boyatzis, and Annie McKee

Process Consultation: Its Role in Organization Development by Edgar Schein

Reframing Organizations Artistry, Choice, and Leadership by Lee G. Bolman and Terrence E. Deal

Straight from the Gut by Jack Welsh

The Benedictine Rule of Leadership by Craig Galbrath

The Certified Six Sigma Black Belt Handbook by Donald W. Benbow and T.M. Kibiak

The Dilbert Principal by Scott Adams

The External Control of Organizations: A Resource Dependence Perspective by J. Pfeffer and G. Selancik

The Fifth Discipline Fieldbook Strategies and Tools for Building a Learning Organization by Peter Senge, Art Kleiner, Charlotte Roberts, Richard Ross, and Bryan Smith

The Fifth Discipline: The Art and Practice of Learning Organizations by Peter Senge

The Five Deficiencies of a Team, a Leadership Fable by Patrick Lencion

The Management and Control of Quality by James R. Evans and William M. Lindsay

The Practice of Management by Peter Drucker

The Time Trap: The Classic Book on Time Management by Alec Mackenzie

The Tipping Point – How Little Things Make a Big Difference by Malcolm Gladwell

Who Moved My Cheese? An Amazing Way to Deal with Change in Your Work and in Your Life by Spencer Johnson

Appendix D – Professional Associations

Obtaining membership in professional associations is an important step to networking and career growth

This is a partial listing for consideration. Contact information and website addresses can be obtained through Internet research. See the website Encyclopedia of Associations for an exhaustive list. Each association will have a national office and regional chapters. Membership criteria and annual dues will differ from one to another.

American Management Association (AMA)

American Society of Association of Executives

American Society of Corporate Secretaries, Inc.

American Society of Training and Development (ASTD)

Association for Corporate Growth

Association of Business Process Management Professionals

Association of Career Professionals

Association of Contingency Planners

Association of Financial Professionals

Association of Health Care Office Management

Association of Proposal Management Professionals

Association of Translation Companies

Association of Work Progress Improvement

Awards & Recognition Association

Business and Professional Women

Business Process Management Group

California Association of Building Energy Consultants

Center for Association Leadership, The

Chartered Institute of Purchasing and Supply, The

Chemical Resources & Management Association

Council of Logistics Management

Council of Supply Chain Management Professionals

Data Management Association

Financial Management Association

Foodservice Management Professionals

HR Policy Association

Human Resource Professionals Association

Institute of Management Accountants

International Association of Administrative Professionals

International Association of Business Communicators (IABC)

International Association of Career Management Professionals

International Association of Professional Communicators

International Customer Service Association

International Guild of Professional Butlers

International Guild of Professional Consultants

International Publishing Management Association

International Society of Six Sigma Professionals

Knowledge Management Professional Society

National Association of Exclusive Buyer Agents

National Association of Legal Secretaries

National Association of Personnel Services

National Association of Restaurant Accountants & Consultants

National Association of State Purchasing Officials

National Black MBA Association

National Contract Management Association

National Council of Real Estate Investment Fiduciaries

National Hispanic Business Association

National Institute of Pension Administrators

National Society of Fund Raising Executives

National Society of Hispanic MBAs

National Wildlife Management Professional Association

Open Source Solutions, Inc.

Paper Industry Management Association

Professional Association Management

Professional Association Management Services

Professional Convention Management Association

Project Management Institute

Public Relations Society of America

Purchasing Management Association of Canada

Records Information Management

Salespeople with a Purpose

Senior Executives Association

Society for Human Resources Management

Society of Competitive Intelligence Professionals

Society of Consumers Affairs Professionals in Business

Texas Association of Physical Plan Administrators

The International Forum

The Moroccan American Business Council

Travel Industry Association of America

United States Council of International Business

Utility Marketing Association

World at Work

Young Presidents' Organization

CITATIONS

1. Imai Masaakiand Gemba Kaizen, *A Commonsense Low-Cost Approach to Management* (New York: McGraw-Hill Professional, 1997), 64.
2. Quote attributed to Machiavelli and Sun Tzu and was used by Michael Cortleone in the *Godfather II* (1974) written by Mario Puzo and directed by Francis Ford Coppola.
3. Dr. Seuss, *Horton Hatches the Egg,* (New York: Random House, 1940)
4. Shingo, S. The Sayings of Shingo, *Key Strategies for Plant Improvement* (Portland: Productivity Press, 1967), 145.
5. Jack Gibb, "TORI Theory, Nonverbal Behavior and the Experience of Community," Gibb Small Group Research, *Sage Journals on Line* (1972), 461-472.
6. Critical Success Factors are known by different names. Each industry develops standards from which performance is measured. As a manager you need to survey the performance of the employees and develop criteria for which data can be collected hourly, daily, or weekly and then publically displayed.
7. G. T. Doran, "There's a S.M.A.R.T. Way to Write Management's Goals and Objectives." *Management Review* 70, (1981), 35-36.
8. Kaoru Ishikawa, *Introduction to Quality Control*, trans. J.H. Loftus, (1990), 448.
9. Richard Beckhard, *Organizational Development Strategies and Models,* (Reading, MA: Addison-Wesley, 1969).
10. Graduate students within a MBA degree courses were polled by the authors of this text regarding their impressions of supervisor − employee performance

evaluation conferences. From their responses the lists of expectations were organized and presented herein.

11. Graduate students within a course "Conflict Management" taught by the author completed an exercise of the identification of the stages of conflict within a work group. The results of their efforts were organized and presented herein.
12. The Change Formula was created by Richard Beckhard and David Gleicher and is called Gleicher's Formula. This formula provides a model to access the relative strengths affecting the likely success of an organizational change program.
13. Richard Beckhard, *Organizational Development: Strategies and Models*, (Reading MA: Addison-Wesley, 1969).
14. F.G. Bolman and Terrance E. Deal, *Reframing Organizations, Artistry, Choice, and Leadership*, 3rd ed, (San Francisco, CA: Josey-Bass A Wiley Imprint, 2003), 241-269.
15. Jeffrey Pfeffer, "Seven Practices of Successful Organizations", *California Management Review*, 40 (Winter 1998), 40, 96-98.
16. Edgar Schein, *Process Consultation, Its Role in Organizational Development,* 1, (New York: Addison-Wesley), 41, 57, 81.
17. Schein's works have defined the role and purpose of process consulting and the value to the organization. In other words the manager is the department's own internal consultant. His writings are highly recommended and are well worth reading.
18. Questions are created by the authors of this book. The questions are intended to focus on an applicant's personal understanding of the values attributed to fulfilling

the role of a manager and the position's performance expectations. Additional questions should be created that explore the managerial and analytical skills of a candidate.

19. The list of ten values was created by the authors of this text. Other terms may be deemed more applicable to a situation at hand. The voting and ranking provides the respondent with the opportunity to select what values are most and least important. From the ranking the manager can identify the values held by the work group.

20. Sun Tzu, <u>The Art of War</u>. The supplemental material written by the authors of this text provides an interpretation of the Sun Tzu passages as applied to the modern business environment. The words of Sun Tzu have a timeless quality that is relevant to the management of organizations. You are encouraged to read and study his writings. As you read take a few moments and take the word "general" and replace it with the word "manager." The replace the word "troops" or " soldiers" with employees and a very interesting managerial philosophy will emerge off of the pages.

www.ingramcontent.com/pod-product-compliance
Lightning Source LLC
Chambersburg PA
CBHW030939180526
45163CB00002B/633